Sweets

Sweets

a collection of *soul food desserts* and *memories*

PATTY PINNER

Photography by Sheri Giblin

Ten Speed Press
Berkeley | *Toronto*

Ten Speed Press
P.O. Box 7123
Berkeley, California 94707
www.tenspeed.com

Distributed in Australia by Simon and Schuster Australia, in Canada by Ten Speed Press Canada, in New Zealand by Southern Publishers Group, in South Africa by Real Books, and in the United Kingdom and Europe by Airlift Book Company.

Jacket and text design by Toni Tajima
Family photos courtesy of the author
Front jacket lower panel photo by Patrick Molnar/Getty Images
Photography by Sheri Giblin
Photo assistance by Jessica Giblin and Guarina Lopez
Food styling by Dan Becker with assistance from Annie Salisbury
Prop styling by Leigh Noë
Recipe testing by Annie Salisbury

Library of Congress Cataloging-in-Publication Data
Pinner, Patty, 1954-
    Sweets: a collection of soul food desserts and memories / Patty Pinner.
        p. cm.
    Includes index.
    ISBN 1-58008-521-0 (alk. paper)
      1. Desserts. 2. African American cookery. I. Title.

TX773.P574 2003
641.8'6—dc21   2003048446

First printing, 2003
Printed in China

1 2 3 4 5 6 7 8 9 10 — 07 06 05 04 03

To Ruth Pinner

Mama, this book wouldn't have been possible if you hadn't had a penchant for preserving recipes and family stories. I'm who I am because of our times together in the kitchen.

To M.C. Pinner

Daddy, psychology is just starting to recognize the importance of a loving father in a girl's life. Because of you, I've known about it all along.

Clockwise from left: Cud'n Madelyn, her husband, Frank, Aint Jessie Mae, Uncle Sam, Pop, unidentified man, My My, Uncle Joe, Aint Helen, Mama, Cud'n Bernice, Cud'n Lionel. Sunday dinner, 1950s.

Contents

Early 1960s, five years old. I was always more observant and more interested in what the grown-ups were talking about than the other kids were. My My said it was because I was an older woman trapped in a young girl's body; she said she could see it in my eyes.

Acknowledgments

Some people live their entire lives not knowing what they were called to do. I thank God for enlightening me when I was a little girl. I thank my son, Craig McAdams, for being a constant source of love and encouragement. I thank my grandmother, Mattie Thompson, whose womanly witticisms still shape, guide, and tickle me. I thank my aunts, Marjell Moore, Helen Arthur, and Betty Jean Sims for their love and support and for always being just a phone call away when I need a quick over-the-phone cooking lesson. I especially thank Aunt Marjell for keeping the family's stories and passing them on. I thank my cousins Larry Moore and Stephanie Brown for helping me locate old family photos. I thank my girlfriends Pamela Wyrick and Susan Howell for encouraging me to tell my family's stories. I thank Rugenia Cooper, an angel God sent all the way from California, to convince me that living in a small town is not always a hindrance to personal aspirations, but sometimes, a launching pad for bigger things to come. I also thank, Patricia El-Amin, Sherry Drain, Rosalinda Matthew, Marilyn Youman, Nora Jackson-Dawkins, Susan Clark, and Thomas Gillespie. Thank you for your constant love, encouragement, and support.

I thank Windy Ferges, Toni Tajima, Aaron Wehner, and Lorena Jones at Ten Speed Press. Windy, thank you for this beautiful book that you've edited and produced. Toni, thank you for designing a lovely book that captures the spirit of my family. Aaron and Lorena, thank you for giving this aspiring author her first break.

Finally, there's the Lisa Ekus Public Relations Company. I thank Rob Dent for all of the editorial assistance that he gave me. I especially thank my agent, Lisa Ekus. Thank you, Lisa, for embracing my manuscript and me from day one. May God cause in you the same joy that you have caused in me.

Saginaw, 1950s. There was never a dull moment on Sixth Street. Somebody colorful was always passing by.

Introduction

According to legend, the Saginaw River is the only river in the world that flows upstream. Because of that peculiarity, and because folks claimed there were two mighty curses put on our little town during its formative years—one inflicted by an irate band of Sauk Indians who became enraged when boorish Michigan lumberjacks trampled all over their sacred burial grounds, and the other by a caravan of visiting gypsies who became incensed when they received a less-than-hospitable welcome from the upstanding citizens of Saginaw—most of the town's tribulations get blamed on either the river, or one of the curses. Regardless of the fact that my maternal grandfather—we called him Pop—accompanied a childhood friend to Saginaw, Michigan, in the summer of 1948 upon hearing that General Motors was hiring and paying well, had my grandmother—we called her My My—known about the curses, she never would have left her native Mississippi a few months later to join my grandfather. There weren't too many things that scared My My, but thunderstorms and curses were at the top of the list of the things that did.

In Saginaw, My My and Pop's first residence was an upstairs room in a boardinghouse owned by an older, heavyset woman named Mother Wiley. They say My My and Mother Wiley got along just fine, except when it came to sharing the boardinghouse's small kitchen. An important part of My My's social life back home had been centered around her reputation as a wonderful cook (her food baskets, and especially her dessert baskets, were highly coveted items at church socials and community events). My My wasn't happy sharing a kitchen (or what it boils down to, sharing her cooking secrets) with Mother Wiley or the other boardinghouse wives who also used the kitchen to cook meals.

My My and Pop soon left Mother Wiley's. They settled a few streets over, into a large Victorian-style house on Sixth Street, in the heart of the black community. My My finally had the run of her own kitchen, the way it had been down South. She loved her new kitchen; she quickly gave it new window treatments and covered the walls with a floral

I

pattern. She kept it immaculate; when the aroma of dinner wasn't wafting out of it, the scent of Pine-Sol was.

When my grandmother first came to Saginaw, she wasn't impressed. She said, "So this is the *Great Up North?* What's so great about it? Folks pass you on the street and they ain't even got sense enough to speak." Eventually, My My would adjust to her new life away from the country. After all, she had four young daughters—Marjell, Helen Marie, Betty Jean, and my mother, Ruth—and a son, Ernest, who were depending on her to help them adapt to this new environment (her eldest, Clarence, had remained down South). As it had been in the South, the church soon became an important part of My My's social life. And just as quickly, her food baskets—especially those holding her desserts—became as popular as they had been in Mississippi.

Like my grandmother, my mother and her sisters were wonderful cooks. My My lovingly shared her cooking secrets with her daughters, believing that if they acquired good kitchen skills it would help them find their way into the hearts of some fine young men—the marrying kind of fine young men.

My father tells me that he met my mother through one of his running buddies; he says his buddy, Eddy Tabron, had an eye on Mama's pretty younger sister, Helen. Daddy says Eddy took him by the house on Sixth Street one day, and he was immediately infatuated with Mama and her family. He says Mama and her sisters were some of the most beautiful and mannerly down-home girls he'd ever met. Daddy, a very handsome bachelor, had been on his own since he was seventeen. He had become accustomed to eating a quick bite here and there. But mealtime in the Thompson household was a spiritual event: it involved a pretty table setting, enticing aromas, southern hospitality, grace before each meal, and My My's scowl if you headed for the dinner table without first heading toward the bathroom faucet and a bar of soap. Daddy was soon eating with Mama and her family every chance he got.

My parents were wed in 1953. My father says it all the time: "I asked Ruth to marry me ten minutes after I met her. She didn't drink, she didn't smoke, and she was beautiful. If I'd'a known how good a cook she was, I'd'a asked her sooner."

By 1960, many of my southern relatives had migrated North. Most of them settled in the bigger cities, like Detroit, Chicago, and Cleveland. However, a few liked the neighborly atmosphere of our small town so much that they decided to lay roots in Saginaw. Big Mama, My My's aunty, was one of the first to settle there.

When I was growing up, the women in my family were the most passionate cooks I knew. They cooked from their hearts and souls. Whether or not they would admit it, they used every meal as an opportunity to flaunt their culinary skills, as an opportunity for prestige and to be noticed, and a chance to further establish themselves in our small town as the queens of soul food. They could really "put their foot" in the meals they cooked (this is what My My would say when someone outdid herself in the kitchen).

To say my family *liked* desserts would be putting it mildly. They *loved* desserts. They collected and guarded their dessert recipes as if they were magic potions. They displayed their treats beneath glass on the tops of freezer chests and antique hutches as if they were displaying the crown jewels. They arrived at fish fries, church dinners, and family gatherings carrying their dessert baskets, pretending to be unaware that their reputation for "putting their foot" in what they cooked had folks anticipating their arrival. It was a sight to see, the queens of soul food (My My, Big Mama, Aint Marjell, Aint Helen, Aint Betty Jean, and Mama) setting up their treats and trying to act like they weren't aware of the spotlight shining on them.

I don't know exactly where they got their love of cooking, but I'm pretty sure it had something to do with my Grandma Annie Loston, who was my maternal great-great-grandmother, Mariah's, mother. Legend has it that Grandma Annie was a slave on a Mississippi plantation. According to the story, Grandma Annie was known throughout the community as the best cook. Folks are said to have come from far and wide for her cakes, pies, and homemade breads because her confections were as beautifully crafted as they were delicious.

When I was growing up in the 1960s, the kitchens in my family belonged to the women. They also served dual purposes. My My's kitchen was where we gathered to discuss family business and it was sacred. My My didn't smoke, she didn't drink, and she didn't cuss—well, not around people who weren't in the family. Her kitchen was our family's headquarters; it was old and countrified, and so clean you could eat off the floor.

Big Mama, My My's aunt on her mother's side, lived around the corner from My My. Big Mama's old-timey kitchen was like the rest of her house—uncomfortably clean. No sooner than you'd put something down, Big Mama was there like lightning to pick it up and dunk it into the hot, sudsy dishwater that stood in her sink from sunup to sundown. Sometimes now, after I've washed the dishes, swept the kitchen floor, and turned the light out because I think my work is done, I picture Big Mama's kitchen, and then I quickly turn the light back on.

Aint Marjell's kitchen was where we got our hair pressed and curled. Divorced with two sons, Aint Marjell worked as a hairdresser to supplement the money she earned as a waitress and a cook at a neighborhood restaurant. There was a steady stream of chatty, ruby-lipped neighborhood women in and out of her kitchen. One corner of her countertop held jars of peachy hair pomades, hot combs, hot comb ovens, and an oval mirror on a stand that magnified your face ten times its normal size. Newly married, Aint Betty Jean had a bright and fanciful kitchen. It was the epitome of the kitchen little girls have in their minds when they play house. On Friday nights the yellow and chrome Formica-topped kitchen table served as a card table for my aunt and uncle and other young couples living in the neighborhood. Aint Helen's kitchen was the most sensual. It was decorated in rich blue tones and exuded the essence of a woman who was dedicated to pleasing her man through his stomach. Her cupboards were full of exotic bottled sauces and all manner of herbs and spices. Hers was the kitchen where my mother and her sisters talked about their men, about loose women who would grin in your face and try to steal your man behind your back, and about the role a clean house and a hearty meal played in keeping a man from straying too far. My mother's large and airy kitchen held a mix of old and new. She collected antiques—lace linens, old pots and pans, odd silver pieces, and Black memorabilia.

Mama made incense and old-fashioned lye soap in her kitchen sink. She washed out our delicates at the sink, grew herbs on the windowsill, and did her ironing in a corner of the kitchen every Monday. She was a cross between a 1950s version of Betty Crocker and a 1960s flower child. It was to Mama's kitchen that we came to find solace when we needed it. Mama had a gift for healing with words of encouragement.

My fondest memories of the women in my family are of them in their various kitchens, clearing their tables and countertops, getting ready to cook. It was magical the way they floated around the room, adding a pinch here, a dash there, a sprinkling here, and a touch there.

Whether it was fried catfish, collard greens and ham hocks, macaroni and cheese, turkey dressing, or pinto beans and smoked neckbones, those were some *cookin'* sisters who loved to show off in the kitchen. They seemed to have been born with the knowledge of just the right stuff to put into their cooking to make it melt in your mouth.

When I think of the foods of my childhood, however, more than the simmering pots of greens and beans, ham hocks, and smoked turkey necks rattling softly on the stove tops, it's the rich and sugary desserts that come to mind, the "sweets" as we called them. No meal seemed complete without something sweet as its grand finale.

It is with love and best wishes that I offer the following soul food dessert recipes from the recipe collections of the women in my family; and it is with love and best wishes that I share my family's stories.

> Some of the following recipes call for an electric mixer, but while electric beaters do come in handy, as my grandmother used to say, "A big spoon and a little determination will do just fine."

Family Tree

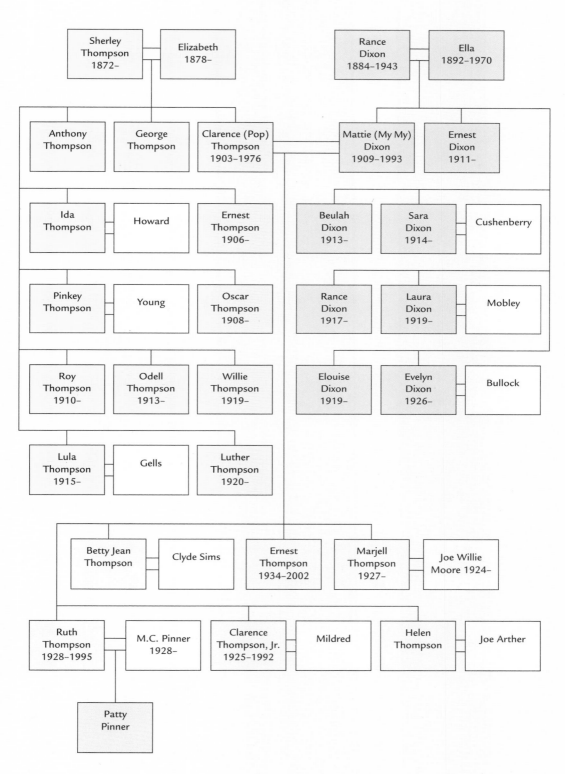

Left to right: Uncle Clyde, Aint Betty Jean, Brother Wiggins (My My's beloved bachelor pastor). At Aint Betty Jean and Uncle Clyde's 1962 wedding, the women in my family prepared all the food—right down to the two wedding cakes My My baked and decorated.

Cakes

Clockwise from left: Mama, family friend Dave, my cousin Larry, Aint Marjell, Pop, Uncle Joe, my cousin Vernise, My My, Aint Helen, Uncle Clyde. Sunday dinner at My My's house, 1960.

When I was a little girl, my cousins and I loved spending Saturday nights in the *old neighborhood* with our grandparents, Pop and My My. I was an only child, and often a lonely child, so having other kids to laugh and play with was a royal treat. My My's house (for some reason we referred to each house in our family, as though it belonged to the woman who resided there) was located on Sixth Street, the major thoroughfare in our community. Sixth Street was to our small town what Beale Street is to Memphis and what Bourbon Street is to New Orleans. It was the heartbeat of *our* community, a winding stretch of concrete abounding with the smells of *our* food, the soulful sounds of *our* music, and the resounding laughter that was the result of the things that tickled *us.* In the summertime, folks walked up and down the street until the wee hours of the morn. In the wintertime, folks still walked up and down the street until the wee hours of the morn.

My My's canary yellow wood-framed house was large and airy. It had lots of nooks and crannies, places for us kids to play and hide. We especially liked the large covered porch that wrapped clear around to the side of the house; we loved jumping off the high banister and onto the freshly mowed lawn down below. Mama and my aunts and uncles would shake their heads and swear that Pop and My My had morphed into different people by the time we came along. "Ain't no way in the world Daddy and Mama would'a let us get away with what they lettin' the grandchildren get away with," they declared. Pop didn't care if we jumped off the banister and onto the lawn as long as we didn't land in his beloved tulip bed. (Pop's tulips were his pride and joy. In early spring, when they were in full bloom, every visit to my grandparents' house ended with Pop giving us a walk through his tulips.)

There was always something exciting going on at My My's house. Aint Betty Jean and Uncle Ernest were teenagers with all of the latest records and a cast of giggling girlfriends and motor-revving dudes coming and going. I don't know who was giving Aint Betty Jean the fever, but when that song "You Give Me Fever" came out, she played the record on the big stereo that sat in the corner of the living room over and over, so much so that its grooves wore down. Uncle Clarence, who was the last of my mother's siblings to migrate North, had taken up residence in a back room. Until we got to know him, he was a curiosity to us children. Just before bedtime, Pop would gather us together on the huge overstuffed sofa and armchairs in the family room and scare us with "down-home" ghost stories, all of which he swore were true. Back then, there were no video games or cable TV; we derived pleasure from simple things.

My My cooked her Sunday dinner every Saturday night. I can still taste the oven-baked barbecued chicken, the rich and creamy macaroni and cheese, the butter rolls, the turnip greens, and the fresh crowder peas, which only needed warming up when we got in from church. Brother Wiggins, our single pastor, came home with us for dinner every Sunday after church. (The women in my family would never admit it, of course, but I know they thought it was because he enjoyed their cooking more than he did that of the other church sisters.)

My My also made her Sunday-dinner sweets on Saturday nights. First, she would make what she called "samples." If the samples were to her liking she would proceed with her baking. If the sample indicated that the pie or cake needed more sugar or spice she would start all over again. Either way, we kids got to eat the samples. She would never make one of anything. There had to be "aplenty" to feed us grandkids, her own kids who might stop by, Brother Wiggins, and anybody else who happened by and wondered, "Whatcha cook sweet today, Miss Mattie?"

Cakes were My My's specialty. It was a talent that she proudly boasted—not in words, but through her manner of displaying the ones she made. She had a large freezer chest on top of which she displayed her cakes on ornate glass cake stands. Sometimes, from a distance, her beautifully iced cakes resembled the spring hats that were on display at her favorite hat shop downtown. When I was a child, atop My My's freezer chest was the first place I looked when I came to visit.

In My My's community down South, cakewalks were very popular. Cakewalks were competitions in which high-stepping, promenading couples competed against each other for the prize of a lovely homemade cake that had been donated by someone in the community. They tell me that when one of My My's cakes was brought to the platform and introduced, couples would suddenly extend the arch in their backs, put a little extra step in their jig, and hasten their trot in the hopes of carrying off one of her beautifully crafted cakes.

My My's

POUND CAKE

Pound cakes are truly a southern dessert. They acquired their name because typically they were made from a pound each of butter, sugar, and flour. My My made the best pound cakes in the world. Her cakes were moist and fragrant confections that rose to delightful heights in the same baking tins that she had used when she lived down South. My My declared that a so-called pound cake that called for anything less than a pound each of the aforementioned was just that—so-called.

To decorate her plain pound cakes, My My would place a fancy paper doily on top of the finished cake, then sprinkle confectioners' sugar over the doily. She would carefully lift the doily and the design would be re-created on the cake.

1 cup (2 sticks) unsalted butter, softened

2½ cups granulated sugar

5 eggs

3 cups cake flour, sifted (My My preferred White Lily or Swan's Down)

1 cup milk

1 teaspoon vanilla extract

Confectioners' sugar (optional)

Preheat the oven to 350°F.

Grease and lightly flour a 10-inch tube pan. Set it aside.

To make the cake, in a large bowl, cream the butter with an electric mixer on medium speed for 2 minutes, or until the mixture is creamy. Gradually add the sugar, beating 5 to 7 minutes, until the mixture is light and fluffy. Add the eggs one at a time, beating well after each addition. Gradually add the flour to the creamed mixture, alternating with the milk; begin and end with the flour. Beat on low speed, just until blended, after each addition. Stir in the vanilla extract. Mix well. Pour the batter into the prepared pan. Bake for 1 hour and 20 minutes, or until a toothpick inserted in the middle of the cake comes out clean. Transfer the cake from the oven to a wire rack. Let it cool in the pan on the rack for 15 minutes. Then run a knife around the inside edge of the pan. Unmold the cake onto the wire rack to cool completely. Transfer the cake to a decorative cake platter and sprinkle with confectioners' sugar, if desired, before serving.

Makes one 10-inch tube cake

My My's
BROWN SUGAR POUND CAKE

My My preferred to serve her sweets on her prettiest china. She believed the delicate patterns on her good china enhanced the flavor of her desserts. This delicious pound cake didn't need fancy china to enhance its flavor. It was scrumptious; it didn't matter if it was served on a piece of china or brought to you on a paper napkin.

The light brown sugar gives this cake a delicate molasses flavor. My My often decorated the top of her brown sugar pound cake with a delicious maple icing. She would brag that even though her fabulous maple icing didn't have to be cooked, it tasted just as good as the kind the "old folks" used to make.

Cake

2 cups firmly packed light
    brown sugar

1 cup granulated sugar

1 cup (2 sticks) unsalted
    butter, softened

¼ cup vegetable shortening

5 eggs

½ teaspoon baking powder

3 cups cake flour (My My
    preferred White Lily or
    Swan's Down brand)

1 cup milk

1 cup chopped pecans

1 tablespoon vanilla extract

Maple Icing

1 (8-ounce) package cream
    cheese, softened

¼ cup (½ stick) unsalted
    butter, softened

4 cups confectioners' sugar,
    sifted

1 teaspoon vanilla extract

½ teaspoon maple-flavored
    extract

Preheat the oven to 350°F.

Grease and lightly flour a 10-inch tube pan. Set it aside.

To make the cake, combine the brown and white sugars, the butter, and the shortening in a large bowl. Cream until the mixture is light and fluffy. Add the eggs one at a time, beating well after each addition. In another large bowl, sift together the baking powder and the flour 3 times. Add the flour mixture to the butter and shortening mixture, alternating with the milk, beginning and ending with the flour. Stir in the pecans and the vanilla extract. Stir until well combined. Pour the batter into the prepared pan. Bake for about 1 hour and 10 minutes, or until a toothpick inserted in the middle of the cake comes out clean. Transfer the cake from the oven to a wire rack. Let the cake cool in the pan for 15 minutes, then unmold it onto the rack to cool completely.

To make the icing, blend together the cream cheese and the butter in a bowl. Stir in the confectioners' sugar. Mix well. Add the vanilla and the maple-flavored extract. Mix until the mixture is smooth. Spread over the cooled cake and transfer to a serving dish.

Makes one 10-inch tube cake

  Sweets

Aint Bulah's
CREAM CHEESE POUND CAKE

Aint Bulah was one of My My's younger sisters. She and her husband, Uncle Wilbur, owned the Community Grocery Store on Louisa Street in New Orleans. By the age of ten, my mama was spending her summers working in Aint Bulah's grocery store, where Mama got to be quite a little businesswoman— keeping the store stocked, sweeping and cleaning, and making sure that folks settled their bills by the last Friday of every month.

Aint Bulah was quite an accomplished "colored" woman for the times; she had a college education and she owned a grocery store. But that still didn't impress her in-laws, who never quite warmed up to her. You see, Aint Bulah had met and married Uncle Wilbur within a week's time. His kinfolk didn't think much of a girl who would do such a thing, despite the fact that the two stayed married for well over fifty years.

This delicious cake was one of Mama's favorite pound cakes for family gatherings because it was large and it served many.

Cake

- 1½ cups (3 sticks) unsalted butter, softened
- 1 (8-ounce) package cream cheese, softened
- 3 cups granulated sugar
- 6 eggs
- 1 tablespoon vanilla extract
- 3 cups cake flour
- 1 (1⅓-ounce) envelope dry whipped topping mix

Glaze

- ½ cup confectioners' sugar, sifted
- 2 teaspoons hot milk
- ¼ teaspoon vanilla extract

Preheat the oven to 325°F.

Lightly grease and flour a 10-inch tube pan. Set it aside.

To make the cake, cream the butter and cream cheese together in a large bowl. Gradually add the sugar. Continue creaming until the mixture is light and fluffy. Add the eggs one at a time, beating well after each addition. Blend in the vanilla extract. Gradually add the flour, beating the mixture until it is smooth. Slowly stir in the whipped topping mix. Stir until well mixed. Pour the batter into the prepared pan. Bake for 1 hour and 30 minutes, or until a toothpick inserted in the middle of the cake comes out clean. Take the cake out of the oven. Let it cool in the pan on a wire rack for 15 minutes, then unmold it onto a wire rack to cool completely. Transfer the cake to a serving platter.

To make the glaze, in a bowl blend the confectioners' sugar, hot milk, and vanilla extract until smooth. Drizzle over the cake.

Makes one 10-inch tube cake

My My's
STRAWBERRY LAYER CAKE

Not only does this cake taste good, it's also a very pretty cake. Its pink color dresses up even the most mundane meal, and its subtle strawberry aroma is divine. When My My brought this cake to the picnic table as the finale to one of our summer get-togethers in her backyard, you could hear our "oohs" and "aahs" echoing throughout the neighborhood.

My My added red food coloring to the frosting—one drop at a time—then she'd blend until she achieved the pink color that she was after.

Cake

1 (18.5-ounce) box white cake
    mix (without pudding)

1 (3-ounce) package
    strawberry Jell-O

1 tablespoon self-rising flour

4 teaspoons granulated sugar

¾ cup vegetable oil

4 eggs

½ cup water

½ of a 10-ounce package
    of frozen strawberries,
    thawed and well drained
    (reserving all the juice and
    the remaining berries)

Strawberry Frosting

Reserved strawberries and
    juice, above

2 (1-pound) boxes
    confectioners' sugar, sifted

½ cup (1 stick) unsalted butter

Red food coloring (optional)

Preheat the oven to 350°F.

Grease and lightly flour three 8-inch round cake pans. Set them aside.

To make the cake, combine the cake mix, Jell-O, flour, and sugar in a large bowl. Mix well. Add the oil. Add the eggs one at a time, beating well after each addition. Add the water and the half package of strawberries to this mixture. Mix well. Divide the batter evenly into the prepared pans. Bake for 25 to 30 minutes, or until a toothpick inserted into the middle of each layer comes out clean and the layers pull away from the sides of the pans. Transfer the layers from the oven to wire racks. Let them cool, still in their pans, for 10 minutes. After 10 minutes, run a knife around the inside edge of each pan, then unmold each layer onto the racks to cool completely.

To make the frosting, in a bowl, combine the remaining strawberries and the reserved juice with the confectioners' sugar and the butter. Beat with a mixer (or mash by hand) until smooth and well blended. Transfer the cake layers, one at a time, onto a serving platter. Frost between each layer, on top of the cake, and around the sides with frosting.

Makes one 8-inch cake

Cakes of My Childhood

The cakes of my childhood were big, rich, and wonderfully moist, and they required the approval of all the women in the family before they were inducted into our family's collection of cherished recipes.

My My brought most of her recipes with her from the South; she carried many of them in her head. Occasionally though, she would call home to one of her cousins or to one of her sisters (Sara, Bulah, Evelyn, Laura, or Eloise) who still lived down South, requesting something "new and different" for an upcoming church supper or a family gathering. My southern great-cousins and great-aunts were as dedicated to their culinary reputations as were their relatives transplanted to the North. The person who had gotten the call from My My would spread the word that the kin up North were on the lookout for a recipe for something good and different. In no time, someone from "home" would call with the perfect recipe.

Mama's

PLAIN CAKE

When I was a little girl we usually had something sweet (made from scratch) in the house; cooking from scratch wasn't a big deal the way it is nowadays. More times than not, that something sweet was a cake. If Mama was in the mood for something quick and easy during the week, she would throw together this plain little cake in no time. Normally Mama would serve this cake plain, but sometimes she'd put a nice little frosting on it—especially if she made it on a day that wasn't her wash day or her ironing day or her grocery-shopping day (back then, folks had certain days set aside for their chores).

1 cup (2 sticks) unsalted butter, softened

2 cups granulated sugar

4 eggs

1 teaspoon vanilla extract

1 teaspoon almond extract

1¼ cups milk

3 cups self-rising flour

Preheat the oven to 350°F.

Grease well, but do not flour, a 9 by 13-inch pan. Set it aside.

In a large bowl, cream the butter and sugar with an electric mixer until they are light and fluffy. Add the eggs one at a time, beating well after each addition. In another bowl, combine the vanilla and the almond extracts with the milk. Blend well. Sift the flour into a large bowl, then add one-third of the flour mixture to the butter and sugar mixture; follow with half of the milk mixture. Beat with the mixer on the slowest speed until the flour is mixed, then add the second third of the flour and the remaining milk. Scrape the bowl down and add the remaining flour. Mix until all of the ingredients are well blended. Pour the batter into the prepared pan. Bake for 40 to 45 minutes, or until a toothpick inserted in the middle of the cake comes out clean. Transfer the cake from the oven to a wire rack to cool completely before cutting the cake into serving squares.

Make one 9 by 13-inch cake

My My's
THREE-LAYER CAKE

My My loved ornate glass cake stands. When we went shopping downtown, the housewares department was the first section of Jacobson's Department Store that we browsed. When the saleslady would ask, "May I help you?" My My would say, "I'm lookin' for something pretty to sit my cakes on."

When I was a little girl, the taller a cake, the more it tantalized me. My My's tall layer cakes were iced with thick, rich layers of frosting, and that made them even more tempting. This cake calls for the flavoring of your choice. Most times My My iced her three-layer cake with an all-purpose vanilla frosting, though you can substitute the vanilla extract in the frosting with almond or lemon extract.

Cake

1 cup (2 sticks) unsalted butter, softened

2 cups granulated sugar

4 eggs, separated

2 teaspoons baking powder

½ teaspoon salt

3 cups all-purpose flour

1 cup milk

2 teaspoons flavoring (extract) of your choice (such as vanilla, almond, or lemon)

Vanilla Frosting

2 cups granulated sugar

⅔ cup all-purpose flour

⅛ teaspoon salt

2 cups evaporated milk

1 teaspoon vanilla extract

1 cup (2 sticks) unsalted butter, softened

Preheat the oven to 375°F.

Grease and lightly flour three 9-inch round cake pans. Set them aside.

To make the cake, cream the butter and sugar together in a large bowl. Mix until fluffy. Add the egg yolks one at a time, beating well after each addition. To the egg yolk mixture, add the baking powder, salt, and 1 cup of the flour. Blend in ⅓ cup of the milk. Alternate adding the remaining flour and the remaining milk, ending with the flour. Add 2 teaspoons of your choice of flavoring. In a large bowl, beat the egg whites until they are stiff (but not dry). Fold the egg whites into the flour mixture using a large spoon or a rubber spatula. Fold just until there are no streaks remaining in the mixture. Divide the batter evenly into the prepared pans. Bake 30 to 35 minutes, or until a toothpick inserted in the middle of each layer comes out clean. Transfer the layers, still in their pans, to wire racks and let them cool for 10 minutes. Unmold the layers onto the wire racks to cool completely.

To make the frosting, in a heavy saucepan, combine the sugar, flour, and salt. Mix well. Slowly whisk in the milk and bring the mixture to a boil over medium heat, stirring constantly. Cook until thick, like bacon grease, about 12 to 15 minutes. The mixture will be a light tan color. Remove from the heat and stir in the vanilla extract. Set aside to cool completely. In a large bowl, beat the butter with an electric mixer until it is light in color and fluffy. Add the cooled mixture and beat until the frosting reaches the spreading consistency of your choice. Frost between the layers, around the sides, and on top of the cake. Transfer the cake to a good-looking serving platter.

Makes one 9-inch cake

BUTTER CAKE

Mmm! Mmm! Delicious. Lots of butter, sugar, and eggs make this cake nice and rich. I like to serve this sweet treat with a dollop of whipped cream or a scoop of vanilla ice cream on top of each slice.

1¼ cups (1½ sticks) unsalted butter, softened

1½ cups granulated sugar

4 eggs

2 cups all-purpose flour

1¼ cups heavy cream

½ tablespoon vanilla extract

1 teaspoon lemon extract

Preheat the oven to 325°F.

Grease and lightly flour a 10-inch tube pan. Set it aside.

In the large bowl, cream the butter and sugar with an electric mixer until fluffy. Add the eggs one at a time, mixing well after each addition. Add the flour, one cup at a time, alternating with the cream, mixing well after each addition. Add the vanilla and lemon extracts and blend well. Pour the batter into the prepared pan. Bake for 1½ hours, or until a toothpick inserted in the middle of the cake comes out clean. Take the cake out of the oven. Let it cool in the pan on a wire cake rack for 15 minutes, then unmold onto the wire rack to cool completely. Transfer to a serving platter.

Makes one 10-inch tube cake

Aint Betty Jean's
CARAMEL CAKE

Aint Betty Jean was Mama's baby sister. I spent a lot of time with Aint Betty Jean when she was a teenager. We'd go to the movies, ride the roller coaster at Winona Beach, and wade in the cool water of the Saginaw Bay at Michigan State Park. Like most teenagers, Aint Betty Jean drove fast. I can still feel the wind blowing in my little face as we whizzed up and down the Bay City Highway in her red Mercury convertible. From where I was sitting in the backseat, I could see the white oversized sunglasses that she wore and the trademark chiffon scarf that she'd wrapped elegantly around her head. Every now and then she would smile at me through the rearview mirror. And I'd feel pure love coming from her. Sometimes we forget to be kind to children. We think they don't have the kind of intelligence that recognizes—and remembers—the source of absolute love. I remember my aunt's love for me in the way she'd hold my hand as we walked along the beach at Winona and in the gentle way she'd carry me at midnight to my waiting parents' arms when I'd tried, but failed again, to spend the entire night away from home. As good as Aint Betty Jean was to me, I still can't figure out what possessed me—I was about five—to open and eat the entire box of Godiva chocolates that her boyfriend brought to the house one day and asked me to give to her when she got home. All these years later, I still regret opening and eating my aunt's entire box of chocolates.

Aint Betty Jean's fabulous caramel cake features three moist yellow cake layers coated in a sweet icing. Like Aint Betty Jean, this luscious caramel cake has always been one of my favorites.

1½ cups (3 sticks) unsalted butter, softened

2 cups granulated sugar

5 eggs

2 teaspoons vanilla extract

3 cups cake flour (Aint Betty Jean prefers Swan's Down brand)

3 teaspoons baking powder

½ teaspoon salt

1 cup milk

Caramel Icing (recipe follows)

Preheat the oven to 350°F.

Grease and lightly flour three 9-inch round cake pans. Set them aside.

To make the cake, in a large bowl, cream the butter and sugar until they are creamy and smooth. Add the eggs one at a time, beating well and scraping down the bowl after each addition. Add the vanilla extract. Mix well. In another bowl, combine the flour, baking powder, and salt. Sift 3 times, then add the sifted flour mixture, alternating with the milk, to the creamed butter mixture. Mix until well combined. Divide the batter evenly into the prepared cake pans. Bake for 25 to 35 minutes, or until a toothpick inserted in the middle of each layer comes out clean. Transfer from the oven to wire racks. Let the layers cool in their pans for 10 minutes, then unmold the layers onto wire racks to cool completely. Transfer the cake layers, one at a time, to a serving platter. Ice between the layers, on top, and on the sides of the cake with Caramel Icing.

Makes one 9-inch cake

Caramel Icing

This is a very old method for making caramel icing. My My taught all of her girls—her daughters and her grands—this old-fashioned recipe, which can be tedious to make. My My used to tell us, "The way to a man's heart is through his stomach . . . and through his eyes and his ears and his nose. Once in a while it's good to let a man see that you're willing to go an extra mile to make things special for him. It makes him feel big. And honey," she would say, narrowing her eyes to emphasize the seriousness of what she was about to add, "don't let nobody tell you nothin' contrary—a man falls in love with a woman based on the way she makes him feel."

2 (12-ounce) cans evaporated milk

2 cups granulated sugar

¼ cup (½ stick) unsalted butter

Combine the milk, sugar, and butter in a heavy saucepan. Cook, stirring frequently (it will scorch if you don't) over low heat for about 2½ hours, or until the mixture is thick and bubbly. Remove from the heat and cool slightly. Frost the cake layers while the icing is still slightly warm.

Clockwise from left: Me, Aint Betty Jean, Uncle Clyde (her fiancé at the time), early 1960s. I used to feel so glamorous sitting in the backseat of Aint Betty's red convertible as we whizzed around town.

Aint Millie's
GRAHAM CRACKER CAKE

Uncle Clarence, Mama's eldest brother, was the last of her siblings to move North. As soon as Uncle Clarence came to town, he got a job working for General Motors. As we kids got to know him, we soon determined that he was rich. We overheard our parents teasing him about his penny-pinching and heard them asking him what he—a single man—was gonna do with all of that G.M. money that he was making. We heard our parents talking among themselves about the municipal bonds and the old coins that he kept locked away in the large army trunk he'd brought his belongings in when he first arrived. We heard our mothers say that he was a good catch because men like him—single, with money put aside—were hard to come by.

We would watch him enter his bedroom at the back of My My's house and hear the lock turn on his door, then we'd sneak closer to listen for sounds that might uncover what this "stranger" was doing. We'd hear the rattle of keys turning the lock on the trunk, and then we'd hear the clatter of heavy coins. We imagined the trunk to be overflowing with gold and silver, coins and jewels.

Eventually, Uncle Clarence became one of our favorite uncles. He didn't have kids of his own to spoil, so he spoiled his nieces and his nephews. We were extremely disappointed when he eventually met, and fell in love with, his wife, Aint Millie—not because we didn't like her, but because we assumed that since she was so sweet and proper, he'd stop spoiling us and start spoiling her.

This delicious, easy-to-make graham cracker cake is what Aint Millie brought to all of our family gatherings. Sometimes she'd already have it covered with cream cheese glaze. Other times, she'd bring a tub of whipped cream and each of us would be responsible for garnishing our own servings. Either way, this cake is full of flavor.

Cake

- 1 cup (2 sticks) unsalted butter, softened
- 2 cups granulated sugar
- 5 eggs
- 1 (16-ounce) box graham crackers, crushed into crumbs
- 2 teaspoons baking powder
- ⅔ cup milk
- 1 (4.5-ounce) can cream of coconut
- 1 cup chopped pecans

Cream Cheese Glaze

- ½ cup (1 stick) unsalted butter, softened
- 1 (3-ounce) package cream cheese, softened
- 2 teaspoons milk, or more as needed
- 1 teaspoon vanilla extract
- 4 cups confectioners' sugar

Preheat the oven to 350°F.

Lightly grease three 9-inch round cake pans. Set them aside.

To make the cake, cream the butter and sugar in a large bowl. Blend until the mixture is very light and fluffy. Add the eggs one at a time, beating after each addition. Add the graham cracker crumbs and the baking powder to the mixture, alternating with the milk. Blend in the cream of coconut and the pecans until the ingredients are evenly distributed. Bake in the prepared cake pans for 35 to 40 minutes, or until a toothpick inserted in the middle of each layer comes out clean. Allow the layers to cool in the pans on wire racks for 10 minutes, then unmold the layers onto the wire racks to cool completely.

To make the glaze, cream the butter and the cream cheese in a bowl until light and fluffy. Add the milk and vanilla extract. Beat until smooth. Gradually add the confectioners' sugar, continuing to beat until smooth and creamy. If necessary, add more milk to reach the desired spreading consistency.

Transfer the cake layers, one at a time, to a serving platter. Frost between the layers, on top, and the sides of the cake with the glaze.

Makes one 9-inch cake

Mama's oldest brother, Uncle Clarence, with his new bride, Aint Millie, mid-1960s.

Cud'n Flossie's
WALNUT WONDER CAKE

Cud'n Flossie was Big Mama's daughter. If you can imagine it, Cud'n Flossie was cleaner than My My, my mother, and every one of my aunts; she was even cleaner than Big Mama, who cleaned her house from sunup to sundown. Cud'n Flossie bathed so often, according to the doctor, she had washed all of the natural oil out of her skin. Whenever we went to visit Cud'n Flossie—she lived in Mississippi—we knew that no matter what time of morning or night we arrived we would be expected to take a long, hot bath before we lay on her snowy white sheets. In fact, while we were still downstairs taking off our coats, Cud'n Flossie was already upstairs running our bathwater.

Our Uncle Sam—Big Mama's brother from Detroit—arrived at Cud'n Flossie's early one morning. No sooner than he'd gotten inside the house good, Cud'n Flossie led him upstairs where she had a hot bath waiting. A while later, when Cud'n Flossie's cat, Opal, unexpectedly nudged open the bathroom door, to Cud'n Flossie's (and Opal's) horror, poor Uncle Sam was sitting on the side of the tub, fully clothed, splashing the bath water as though he were taking a bath. It hadn't dawned on him that nosy Opal might bust in on him and expose his little ruse. It wasn't that Uncle Sam was against bathing, but the poor man was getting on in age, he'd been bumping up and down on a bus all day and all night, and by the time he got to Mississippi he was plum wore out. Needless to say, the next time Uncle Sam went South, he stayed with Cud'n Minnie. Cud'n Minnie had a lot of virtues, but cleanliness wasn't one of them.

They say Cud'n Flossie couldn't keep a man because of her cleanliness; they say it ran them all away. Mama used to say, "Sometimes a woman can be too clean for her own good."

One of the wonderful things about this moist, pretty cake is that you bake and serve it in the same pan. There aren't a lot of dishes involved, so there's not a lot of mess to clean up.

Cake

1 cup (2 sticks) unsalted butter, softened

1 cup granulated sugar

2 eggs

1 teaspoon vanilla extract

2 cups cake flour

½ teaspoon salt

1 teaspoon baking powder

1 teaspoon baking soda

1 cup sour cream

Whipped cream (optional)

Walnut Layer

1½ cups chopped walnuts

½ cup firmly packed brown sugar

6 tablespoons granulated sugar

1½ teaspoons ground cinnamon

Preheat the oven to 350°F.

Lightly grease and flour a 9 by 13-inch pan. Set it aside.

To make the cake, cream the butter and sugar together in a large bowl. Beat in the eggs and vanilla extract. Set aside. In another large bowl, sift together the flour, salt, baking powder, and baking soda. Combine the flour mixture into the butter mixture, alternating with the sour cream.

To make the walnut layer, combine the walnuts, brown and white sugars, and cinnamon in a bowl. Mix until well combined.

Spread half of the cake batter in the prepared pan. Top with half of the walnut layer. Add the remaining batter, then top with the remaining walnut layer. Bake for 45 minutes, or until the top of the cake is nicely browned. Transfer the cake from the oven to a wire rack. Let it cool for 10 minutes. Serve with a dollop of whipped cream on top of each portion, if desired.

Makes one 9 by 13-inch cake

Left, Cud'n Flossie; *right,* Po' Cud'n Ophelia, Mississippi, early 1960s. My My's cousin Flossie had a reputation for being too clean; Pop's cousin Ophelia had one for being too independent.

SUNDAY MORNIN' COFFEE CAKE

Yellow cake mix and Jell-O pudding mix make this an appetizing cake that goes well with a cup of coffee and the Sunday paper. Butter extract provides a buttery flavor to the cake. I prefer the Watkins brand, which can be purchased at their website, www.watkinsonline.com.

Cake

½ cup firmly packed brown sugar

1½ teaspoons ground cinnamon

½ cup chopped pecans

1 (18.5-ounce) box yellow cake mix

1 (6-ounce) package instant vanilla Jell-O pudding mix

1 cup plain yogurt or sour cream

¾ cup hot water

4 eggs

⅓ cup vegetable oil

1 teaspoon vanilla extract

1 teaspoon butter extract

Brown Sugar Icing

⅓ cup firmly packed brown sugar

1½ tablespoons flour

¼ cup (½ stick) unsalted butter, softened

½ cup milk or heavy cream

2 tablespoons brandy or rum

¼ teaspoon vanilla extract

Preheat the oven to 350°F.

Grease and lightly flour a 9 by 13-inch pan. Set it aside.

To make the cake, combine the brown sugar, cinnamon, and pecans in a mixing bowl. Mix well. Set the bowl aside. In a large bowl, combine the cake mix, pudding mix, sour cream, and hot water. Mix well. Beat in the eggs, vegetable oil, vanilla extract, and butter extract; beat until no lumps remain. Pour half of the batter into the prepared pan. Sprinkle with half of the brown sugar and nut mixture, being careful to evenly distribute over the entire surface of the cake batter. Carefully spread the remaining batter over the brown sugar and nut mixture, then sprinkle with the remaining brown sugar and nut mixture. Bake for 35 to 40 minutes, or until a toothpick inserted in the middle of the cake comes out clean. Remove the cake from the oven and cool slightly.

To make the icing, combine the sugar and the flour in a bowl. Set the bowl aside. Over medium heat, melt the butter in a large, heavy saucepan. Whisk the flour and sugar mixture into the melted butter, just until the mixture becomes moistened. Decrease the heat to low. Continue to cook, stirring occasionally, for 2 minutes, or until the mixture becomes slightly stringy. Stir in the milk. Raise the heat to medium and cook until the mixture becomes thick and smooth, stirring frequently. After 5 minutes, stir in the brandy and vanilla extract. Remove the icing from the heat and let it cool to lukewarm. Drizzle over the warm coffee cake.

Makes one 9 by 13-inch cake

Girlfriends

Even though My My was a church-going woman with lots of church-going lady friends, her best friends were Miss Emma Brenyak and Miss LaLou. Both women lived in the neighborhood, in big, immaculate houses just like My My's. Miss Emma, who looked and talked like Pearl Bailey, owned the dry cleaner around the corner from My My's house. She was an ample-sized woman who wore high-heeled pumps and close-fitting dresses and called everybody "Baby Doll." She swished when she walked; you could hear the rustle of silk beneath her dresses.

Miss LaLou lived across the street and was the most delightful woman I knew. A cross between Lucille Ball and Josephine Baker, she was tall and slim and wore a variety of big red wigs, loud perfumes, and noisy bracelets that made jingling sounds on her skinny wrists. Miss LaLou—who drove a white Cadillac with fins protruding in the back—would sit on her porch in the summertime with her white poodle, Sugar, and a glass of scotch and water, smiling seductively

(continued)

Left to right: Miss Emma Brenyak, Miss Beatrice, My My, Miss Cora Belle, early 1960s. My My relished having her girlfriends over for coffee and cake.

(continued from page 27)

at the men who passed by. When the women in my family talked behind Miss LaLou's back, they said she was a fast and scandalous old woman *who needed to go somewhere and sit down.* They accused her of purposely letting Sugar roam the front yard so that she could strike up a conversation with the men she startled, the ones who'd be passing by and think she was talking to them when she'd call out, "Come here, Sugar! Come to Mama." I thought Miss LaLou was charming.

Neither Miss Emma or Miss LaLou came around every day—My My said that any woman who came to her house every day wasn't gettin' her work done at home and was keeping My My from getting hers done, too.

When My My's matronly church-going lady friends—Sister Rose Johnston, Miss Essie Brazil, Fannie Mae Watts, or Miss Cora Bell Haines—stopped by, she and Pop entertained them on the big front porch or in the family room with homemade ice tea or fresh-squeezed lemonade. But when Miss Emma Brenyak or Miss LaLou came around, My My had this certain look that she gave Pop, then he would gather up his things and go into another room. My My used to say that you couldn't keep a man from runnin' around if that's what he wanted to do. "But you sho' ain't got to help him wit' it by supplying him with the women."

It didn't matter if they were sanctified in the Holy Ghost, wore silk beneath their close-fitting dresses, or sat on their front porches drinking scotch and water, My My's girlfriends loved her pretty cakes. Their eyes brightened when she'd take a tray containing her rose-patterned china and slices of one of her cakes into the family room or onto the front porch; it was an instant celebration.

Cud'n Ida Belle's
OLD-FASHIONED SPICE CAKE

Cud'n Ida Belle loved wide-brimmed hats the way Imelda Marcos loved shoes. They say Cud'n Ida—who wasn't much to look at in the face—reveled in the only attention that she got, which was on Sunday mornings when she walked through the church door wearing one of her fancy hats. They say her hats were so wide she had to turn sideways to get through the door. Cud'n Ida Belle and her husband, Cud'n Silas, lived in a two-room shack in the backwoods of Mississippi. Actually, they say Cud'n Ida Belle and Cud'n Silas lived in one of the rooms and that Cud'n Ida Belle's wide-brimmed hats lived in the other, that's how many she had.

Most times, we served Cud'n Ida Belle's cake with a maple sugar frosting, but it tastes just as good with a lemon glaze or a rich chocolate frosting.

Cake

½ cup (1 stick) unsalted butter, softened

1½ cups granulated sugar

3 large eggs

1 cup buttermilk

½ cup orange juice

2½ cups all-purpose flour

1½ teaspoons baking soda

1 teaspoon salt

1 teaspoon ground cinnamon

½ teaspoon ground allspice

½ teaspoon ground ginger

⅛ teaspoon ground nutmeg

1 cup chopped pecans

2 tablespoons grated orange zest

1 teaspoon orange extract

1 teaspoon vanilla extract

Maple Sugar Frosting

2 cups confectioners' sugar, sifted

¾ cup firmly packed dark brown sugar

½ cup (1 stick) unsalted butter, softened

⅛ teaspoon salt

½ cup maple syrup

1 teaspoon vanilla extract

3 tablespoons milk, or more as needed

Preheat the oven to 350°F.

Lightly grease and flour three 9-inch round cake pans. Set them aside.

To make the cake, in a large bowl beat the butter with an electric mixer on medium-high speed until it's light and fluffy. Gradually add the sugar, beating the mixture until it is well combined and smooth. Decrease the mixer speed to medium, then add the eggs one at a time, beating well and scraping down the bowl after each addition. In another bowl, combine the buttermilk and orange juice. Mix well, then set aside. In another bowl, combine the flour, baking soda, salt, cinnamon, allspice, ginger, and nutmeg. Mix until well blended. Add the flour mixture to the butter mixture, alternating with the

(continued)

(continued from page 29)

buttermilk mixture. Begin and end with the flour mixture. Mix on low speed after each addition until well blended. Stir in the pecans, grated orange zest, and orange and vanilla extracts. Stir until just combined. Divide the batter evenly into the prepared pans. Bake for 25 to 30 minutes, or until a toothpick inserted in the middle of each layer comes out clean. Take the layers out of the oven. Let them cool for 10 minutes, in their pans, on wire racks. Unmold the layers onto the wire racks to cool completely.

To make the frosting, in a bowl combine the confectioners' sugar, brown sugar, butter, and salt. Beat with an electric mixer on medium speed until well blended. Continue beating the mixture while gradually adding the maple syrup in a steady stream. Add the vanilla extract and the milk. Increase the mixer speed to medium-high and continue to beat until light and airy. Add another tablespoon of milk if necessary to achieve a spreadable consistency. Transfer the cake layers, one at a time, onto a serving platter. Frost between each layer, on top of the cake, and around the sides with frosting.

Makes one 9-inch cake

Left to right: Cud'n Ida Belle, Aint Laura, Uncle Rance, My My. Rural Mississippi, 1950s.

Li'l Mama's
APPLESAUCE SHEET CAKE

"Li'l Mama" was what we called My My's mother. During the Christmas holidays, Li'l Mama would airmail us a gigantic cardboard box containing her homemade cookies, cakes, and pies. Li'l Mama's Christmas boxes always contained a bag of fat peppermint sticks for us kids and a tin full of horehound candy for the adults. It was such a treat when Mr. Carter, the postman, backed his jeep into My My's driveway, then came to the door with the message, "Y'all got a box from back home." Pop would accept the heavily taped box, then carry it to the dining room table. The words FRAGILE, HANDLE WITH CARE, written in Li'l Mama's scribbly handwriting, were blazed all over the box. It was such a treat to gather around Pop as he was cutting open one of Li'l Mama's Christmas boxes. Talk about anticipation!

This cake stays moist for days. The foolproof walnut–cream cheese frosting is the perfect match for this country cake.

Cake

1½ cups applesauce

2 cups granulated sugar

1 cup vegetable oil

4 eggs

2 cups all-purpose flour

2 teaspoons baking soda

1 teaspoon ground cinnamon

¼ teaspoon ground cloves

½ teaspoon salt

Walnut–Cream Cheese Frosting

5 tablespoons unsalted butter, softened

1 (3-ounce) package cream cheese, softened

1 teaspoon vanilla extract

1¾ cups confectioners' sugar, sifted

3 teaspoons milk

1 cup walnuts, finely chopped

Preheat the oven to 350°F.

Lightly grease and flour a 10 by 15-inch baking pan. Set it aside.

To make the cake, combine the applesauce, sugar, and vegetable oil in a large mixing bowl. Blend well. Add the eggs one at a time, beating well after each addition. In another large bowl, combine the flour, baking soda, cinnamon, cloves, and salt. Mix well. Gradually add the flour mixture to the applesauce mixture, mixing well after each addition. Pour the batter into the prepared pan. Bake for 40 to 45 minutes, or until a toothpick inserted in the middle of the cake comes out clean. Let the cake cool for 10 to 15 minutes before frosting.

To make the frosting, in a large mixing bowl, cream together the butter, cream cheese, and vanilla extract until smooth. Gradually add the confectioners' sugar. Mix well. Stir in the milk gradually until the frosting reaches the desired spreading consistency. Frost the cake, then sprinkle with walnuts. Allow the frosted cake to cool completely before cutting it into squares.

Makes one 10 by 15-inch cake

Aint Evelyn's
BANANA CAKE

Aint Evelyn: *You think you'll ever marry again?*

Me: *No, M'am. It doesn't look like it.*

Aint Evelyn: *Why not?*

Me: *Well, they say there's a shortage of eligible men; I won't settle for just anything.*

Aint Evelyn: *Who says there's a shortage of eligible men?*

Me: *It's on the cover of every magazine; the newspaper just did an entire series on it; and that's all they're talkin' about on the talk shows. They're all sayin' there's a shortage of men.*

Aint Evelyn: *Well, that ain't what it says in the Bible. In the Word it says, "Not one shall lack her mate." Now what you go'n believe? What they say, or what God says?*

The banana—cream cheese frosting really sets this cake off, but a nice lemony glaze tastes just as good. Depending on how I feel, I sometimes add a cup of finely chopped nuts to the batter. For a rich banana flavor, the bananas used in this recipe must be ripe.

Cake

1 cup (2 sticks) unsalted butter, softened

2 cups granulated sugar

2 eggs

1 teaspoon vanilla extract

3 cups cake flour

1 teaspoon baking soda

2 teaspoons baking powder

¾ cup milk

1½ cups mashed ripe bananas

1 cup walnuts, finely chopped (optional)

Banana—Cream Cheese Frosting

¼ cup (½ stick) unsalted butter, softened

1 (12-ounce) package cream cheese, softened

1 ripe banana, mashed

¼ teaspoon freshly grated nutmeg

2 teaspoons vanilla extract

3 tablespoons cream or milk

1 (1-pound) box confectioners' sugar

Preheat the oven to 350°F.

Grease and lightly flour three 9-inch round cake pans. Set them aside.

To make the cake, cream the butter, sugar, eggs, and vanilla extract in a large bowl. Set the bowl aside. In another large bowl, sift together the flour, baking soda, and baking powder. Add the flour mixture to the butter and sugar mixture, alternating with milk, beginning and ending with the flour mixture. Fold in the bananas. Mix until the batter is smooth. Stir in the walnuts until they are well distributed. Divide the batter evenly into the prepared cake pans. Bake for 25 to 35 minutes, or until the cake springs

back when lightly touched. Transfer the layers from the oven to wire racks. Let them cool in the pans for 10 minutes, then unmold them onto the racks to cool completely.

To make the frosting, blend the butter, cream cheese, and banana in a large bowl. Add the nutmeg. Mix well. Add the vanilla extract and the cream. Beat until light and fluffy. In another large bowl, sift the confectioners' sugar. Add the sifted sugar to the cream cheese mixture. Mix well, until fluffy. Keep refrigerated until ready to frost the cake.

Transfer the cake layers, one at a time, to a serving platter. Frost between the layers, on top, and on the sides of the cake.

Note: The pinch of grated nutmeg *makes* the frosting.

Makes one 9-inch cake

Clockwise from upper left: My cousins Larry and Jerry, my cousin Freddy, me. All of our birthdays were celebrated with homemade cakes; this photo was taken at my third birthday bash.

Miss Essie Brazil's
THREE-LAYER COCONUT CAKE

Miss Essie was a stout little churchwoman with short, thin hair, protruding front teeth, and a high, cackling laugh that you could hear coming toward you from way up the street. Miss Essie had a knack for quoting Scripture and for keeping track of what was going on in the neighborhood. Although My My wasn't prone to gossip, like anyone else she enjoyed a bit of hearsay now and then. Sometimes in the summertime, when you could hear Miss Essie coming up the street—speaking to the people on their porches and gathering information as she was coming—My My would ease out to the porch with her feather duster in hand. Once she got Miss Essie started, all My My had to say to keep her going was, "Sho'nuff? Shoooo'nuff?" Miss Essie prefaced all of her juicy tidbits with, "Now, you didn't get this from Sister Essie, but what I'm fixin' to tell ya is what God loves . . . and we all know what God loves, God loves the truth."

For variation, you can toast the coconut in this recipe to a golden brown. But a true soul food coconut cake is always snowy white.

Cake

1 cup (2 sticks) unsalted
    butter, softened

2 cups granulated sugar

4 eggs, separated

3 cups cake flour, sifted

2 teaspoons baking powder

¼ teaspoon salt

1 cup milk

1 cup sweetened flaked
    coconut

2 teaspoons vanilla extract

Coconut Frosting

2 cups granulated sugar

¼ cup light corn syrup

1 cup boiling water

3 egg whites

1 teaspoon vanilla extract

2 cups sweetened flaked
    coconut, for garnish

Preheat the oven to 350°F.

Grease and lightly flour three 9-inch round cake pans. Set them aside.

To make the cake, in a large mixing bowl, cream the butter and sugar thoroughly until light and creamy. Add the egg yolks one at a time, beating well after each addition. In a large bowl, sift together the flour, baking powder, and salt. Add the flour mixture to the butter and sugar mixture, alternating with the milk, beating after each addition. Stir in the coconut and the vanilla extract. In another bowl, beat the egg whites until they form stiff peaks. Fold them into the batter. Divide the batter evenly into the prepared cake pans. Bake for 30 minutes, or until a toothpick inserted in the middle of each layer comes out clean. Transfer the layers from the oven to wire racks. Allow them to cool in their pans for 10 minutes, then unmold them onto the wire racks to cool completely.

To make the frosting, in a large saucepan, combine the sugar, corn syrup, and boiling water. Bring to a boil over medium-low heat, and cook until the mixture spins thread and reaches 242°F on a candy thermometer. In a large

(continued)

(continued from page 34)

bowl, beat the egg whites until they form stiff peaks. Pour the sugar and syrup mixture over the egg whites, beating constantly. Add the vanilla extract, then cool the mixture until firm enough to spread.

Transfer one cake layer to a serving platter; spread one-third of the coconut frosting on top. Sprinkle coconut on top. Top with another cake layer and spread with the second third of the frosting. Sprinkle more coconut on top. Top with the remaining cake layer, then spread the remaining frosting over the top and sides of the cake. Sprinkle with the remaining coconut, pressing it gently into the frosting if you want to.

Makes one 9-inch cake

Miss Emma Brenyak's
EASY COCONUT CAKE

This cake is good and easy to make. My My used to say, "In the country, when you went to somebody's house and they brought out a coconut cake, you took it as a sign of welcoming."

1 (18.5-ounce) box white cake mix

1⅓ cups sweetened condensed milk (Miss Emma used Eagle Brand)

¾ cup cream of coconut

1 (9-ounce) tub Cool Whip

½ cup sweetened flaked coconut

Make the cake following the directions on the box. While the cake is still hot, punch holes in the top of it with a large fork. In a bowl, mix the condensed milk and cream of coconut thoroughly with an electric mixer, then pour over the hot cake. Let the cake cool. Just before serving, top with Cool Whip, then sprinkle coconut on top.

Makes one cake

Cud'n Bay Bay's
HONEY CAKE

Cud-n Bay Bay, a distantly related but much-loved cousin of Mama's, had an answer waiting for those who wanted to know why in the world she had married a man twenty years her senior: "The best broth comes from an old pot," she'd say.

This deliciously light and spicy down-home cake calls for a yellow cake mix.

Cake

1 (18.5-ounce) box yellow cake mix

¾ cup vegetable oil

4 eggs

1 cup sour cream

¼ cup honey

1 cup firmly packed brown sugar

1 tablespoon ground cinnamon

¼ teaspoon ground nutmeg

⅛ teaspoon ground cloves

Vanilla Icing

2 cups confectioners' sugar, sifted

4 tablespoons milk, or more as needed

1 tablespoon vanilla extract

Preheat the oven to 325°F.

To make the cake, combine the cake mix, vegetable oil, eggs, and sour cream in a large mixing bowl. Mix the ingredients until the majority of the large lumps in the batter are gone. Gently stir in the honey. Pour half of the batter into an ungreased 9 by 13-inch glass cake pan. In a bowl, blend the brown sugar, cinnamon, nutmeg, and cloves. Sprinkle the brown sugar mixture on top of the batter in the cake pan. Pour or spoon the other half of the batter into the cake pan, covering the brown sugar mixture. Bake for 50 minutes, or until a toothpick inserted in the middle comes out clean and the cake is golden brown. Transfer the cake from the oven to a wire rack. Let the cake stand for 10 minutes.

To make the icing, combine the confectioners' sugar, milk, and vanilla extract in a large bowl. Whisk the ingredients until they are smooth. (Add a few more drops of milk if necessary to make the icing thin enough to drizzle onto the cake from a spoon.) Drizzle the icing onto the warm cake.

Makes one 9 by 13-inch cake

Mama's
PINEAPPLE UPSIDE-DOWN CAKE

The women in my family wouldn't cook in a cast-iron skillet until it had been well seasoned; to do otherwise, they claimed, hindered the flavor of the food. Mama seasoned a new skillet by giving it a washing in warm soapy water. After thoroughly drying the skillet by hand, she placed it over a low flame for about two to three minutes to remove all of the moisture. She would let the skillet cool to the touch, then she'd put about two tablespoons of vegetable oil in it (not butter or bacon fat, because animal fats go rancid), after which she'd coat its entire surface using her fingers. The next step was to put the oiled skillet in a preheated 350°F oven for about 30 minutes. After that, she'd let the skillet cool to room temperature. A well-seasoned skillet was one that she'd put through this process several times.

This country classic was one of Mama's weekday treats. It's not only tasty, it's also quick and easy to prepare.

¼ cup (½ stick) unsalted butter

1 cup firmly packed brown sugar

1 (20-ounce) can sliced pineapple

10 maraschino cherries

1 cup all-purpose flour, sifted

1 teaspoon baking powder

¼ teaspoon salt

3 eggs, separated

1 cup granulated sugar

½ teaspoon vanilla extract

Preheat the oven to 350°F.

Melt the butter in a well-seasoned 10-inch cast-iron skillet. Remove the skillet from the heat. Sprinkle the brown sugar evenly over the melted butter. Drain the pineapple slices well, reserving 5 tablespoons of the juice. Arrange the drained pineapple slices in a single layer on top of the brown sugar mixture. Place a cherry in the center of each slice. Set the skillet aside. In a large bowl combine the flour, baking powder, and salt. Set the bowl aside. In another large mixing bowl, beat the egg yolks on medium speed until they are thick and lemon colored. Gradually add the granulated sugar to the egg yolks, continuing to beat. Stir in the vanilla extract and the reserved pineapple juice. Mix well. Add the flour mixture to the egg yolk mixture. Mix until well blended. In a large bowl, beat the egg whites until stiff peaks form. Fold the egg whites into the batter, using downward strokes into the bowl. Pour or spoon the batter evenly over the pineapple slices in the skillet. Bake for 35 minutes, until the top is browned and a toothpick inserted in the middle of the cake comes out clean. Let the cake stand in the skillet for 30 minutes, then unmold onto a serving platter. Serve warm or cold.

Makes one 10-inch cake

Sister Rose Johnston's
STRAWBERRY JAM CAKE

This delicious, moist, and tangy country cake was Pop's favorite. We called it "jelly cake." Sister Johnston, who made the best jelly cakes, would drop one off at the house for no particular reason. Sister Johnston was always doing something nice for somebody. Some folks said she did nice things for people so that nice things would be said about her, sort of a give me my flowers while I'm yet breathin' manner of thinking. Other folks said that that just wasn't so; they said Sister Johnston was indeed called to the duty of kindness.

---

1 cup (2 sticks) unsalted butter, softened

2 cups granulated sugar

1 teaspoon vanilla extract

5 eggs

1 teaspoon baking soda

1 cup buttermilk

4 cups cake flour

½ teaspoon salt

1 teaspoon ground cinnamon

1 teaspoon ground nutmeg

1 teaspoon ground allspice

1 teaspoon ground ginger

1 cup chopped pecans

1 (18-ounce) jar strawberry jam

Confectioners' sugar, for dusting

Preheat the oven to 350°F.

Grease and lightly flour three 9-inch round cake pans. Set them aside.

To make the cake, in a large bowl, cream the butter, sugar, and vanilla extract until light and fluffy. Add the eggs one at a time, beating the mixture well after each addition. In a small bowl, stir the baking soda into the buttermilk. Set aside. In another bowl, sift together the flour, salt, cinnamon, nutmeg, allspice, and ginger. Add the dry ingredients, alternating with the buttermilk, to the creamed butter and sugar mixture, beginning and ending with the dry ingredients; mix well. Fold in the pecans and ¾ cup of the jam. Set the remainder of the jam aside. Mix well. Divide the batter evenly into the prepared cake pans. Bake for 35 minutes, or until a toothpick inserted in the middle of each layer comes out clean. Remove from the oven. Cool the layers in the pans on wire racks for 10 minutes, then unmold the layers onto wire racks to cool completely.

After the layers have completely cooled, transfer each layer, one at a time, to a serving platter, spreading the remaining strawberry jam between each layer and on top of the cake. Spread the jam ¼ to ½ inch away from the cake's edges. Garnish the top of the cake with confectioners' sugar. (I sprinkle confectioners' sugar between the layers as well.)

Makes one 9-inch cake

Aint Helen's
SWEET POTATO CHEESECAKE

Months before I got married, I bought a marbled black-and-white spiral notebook and drove thirty-five miles every Saturday morning to my Aint Helen's house to learn how to cook for a man. If anybody had a knack for knowing how to feed a man, the inner man as well as the outer, it was Aint Helen. All my life I'd watched Aint Helen charm her way into her beloved husband's heart through his stomach . . . and his eyes, and his ears, and his nose, using the seductive power of food. She combined thick, manly cuts of meat, exotic and zesty gravies and red sauces, and tantalizing sweet treats with the magic of old-fashioned feminine enchantments—pretty gingham curtains, lacy tablecloths, china cream and sugar bowls, and loving conversation at the table. All one had to do was see the approving look on Uncle Joe's face as he was sitting at the kitchen table to know that a kitchen was capable of being much more than just a place to eat; if a woman knew what she was doing, it was also a place to create magic.

The scrumptious maple-pecan glaze on this cheesecake makes it stand out.

Cake

1¼ cups graham cracker crumbs

¼ cup granulated sugar

¼ cup (½ stick) unsalted butter, softened

3 (8-ounce) packages cream cheese, softened

1 (14-ounce) can sweetened condensed milk

2 cups mashed cooked sweet potatoes

3 eggs

¼ cup maple syrup

1½ teaspoons ground cinnamon

1 teaspoon ground nutmeg

½ teaspoon salt

Maple Pecan Glaze

¾ cup maple syrup

1 cup heavy cream

½ cup chopped pecans

Preheat the oven to 350°F.

Lightly grease the bottom and sides of a 9-inch springform pan. Set it aside.

To make the crust, combine the graham cracker crumbs, granulated sugar, and butter in a large bowl. Stir until well blended. Press the crust firmly into the bottom and 1 inch up on the sides of the prepared pan.

To make the filling, in a large bowl, beat the cream cheese with an electric mixer on medium speed until light and fluffy. Add the condensed milk and beat until smooth. Add the sweet potatoes to the cream cheese mixture, then blend until smooth. Add the eggs one at a time, beating well after each addition. Add the maple syrup, cinnamon, nutmeg, and salt, beating until blended. Pour the filling over the crust. Bake for 60 to 75 minutes, or until set.

Turn the oven off when the filling is set. Partially open the oven door and let the cheesecake stand in the oven for about 1 hour. After 1 hour, remove the cake from the oven and carefully run a small knife around the rim of the pan to loosen the cake. Transfer the cake to a wire rack. Refrigerate the cake, still in its pan, overnight. The next day, remove the rim of the pan from the cheesecake.

  Sweets

To make the glaze, in a saucepan, combine the maple syrup and cream. Bring to a boil over medium heat, stirring often, until the mixture thickens, about 15 minutes. Fold in the pecans. Remove the saucepan from the burner to cool completely. Spoon the topping over the cooled cheesecake just before serving.

Makes one 9-inch cake

Uncle Joe and Aint Helen, 1950s. Aint Helen was the most sensuous cook that I knew.

Aint Laura's

YAM CAKE

Aint Laura was My My's sister. She was a licensed beautician who lived in New Orleans. Like most "colored" women of that era (the '30s, the '40s, and the '50s), she used her kitchen as her beauty parlor. When Mama was a little girl and had free time away from her job at Aint Bulah's grocery store, Aint Laura would pay Mama a quarter to sweep the kitchen floor. Aint Laura was particular about keeping her floors clean and free of hair. She didn't want her customers going around accusing her of keeping their hair to "work roots" on them in order to keep their business. Nor did she want them accusing her of selling their hair to their boyfriends' wives or to their husbands' mistresses, the way it was rumored that some beauticians did.

The orange icing gives this yam cake its zest—no play on words intended.

Cake

2 cups granulated sugar

1½ cups vegetable oil

4 eggs

2 cups all-purpose flour, sifted

2 teaspoons baking powder

1 teaspoon baking soda

1 teaspoon salt

2 teaspoons ground cinnamon

¼ teaspoon ground nutmeg

⅛ teaspoon ground cloves

3 cups grated raw yams

1 tablespoon vanilla extract

1 cup pecans, finely chopped

Orange Icing

⅓ cup unsalted butter, softened

¼ cup orange juice

1½ tablespoons grated orange zest

Pinch of salt

½ teaspoon vanilla extract

½ teaspoon orange extract

3 cups confectioners' sugar, sifted

Preheat the oven to 350°F.

Thoroughly grease and flour three 9-inch round cake pans. Set them aside.

To make the cake, in a large bowl, cream the sugar and vegetable oil until they are well blended. Add the eggs one at a time, beating well after each addition; set the bowl aside. In another large bowl, sift together the flour, baking powder, baking soda, salt, cinnamon, nutmeg, and cloves. Add the flour mixture to the sugar mixture, adding a little at a time. Mix well after each addition. Fold in the yams, vanilla extract, and pecans. Divide the batter evenly into the prepared cake pans. Bake for 45 to 50 minutes, or until a toothpick inserted in the middle of each layer comes out clean. Remove the layers from the oven. Let them cool in their pans on wire racks for 10 minutes. Remove the cake layers from the pans, unmolding them onto the wire racks to cool completely.

To make the icing, combine the butter, orange juice, orange zest, salt, and vanilla and orange extracts in a large bowl. Mix thoroughly. Gradually beat in the confectioners' sugar, adding a little at a time. Beat the mixture until it is smooth and creamy.

Transfer the cake layers, one at a time, onto a serving platter. Frost between each layer, on top of the cake, and around the sides with the icing.

Makes one 9-inch cake

Aint Marjell's
7-UP CAKE

Unlike most 7-Up cakes, Aint Marjell's cake is made in a Bundt pan.

1½ cups (3 sticks) unsalted butter, softened

3 cups granulated sugar

5 eggs

3 cups all-purpose flour

1 teaspoon lemon extract

1 teaspoon vanilla extract

¾ cup 7-Up

Confectioners' sugar, for dusting

Preheat the oven to 325°F.

Grease and lightly flour a 10-inch tube pan. Set it aside.

In a large bowl, cream the butter and sugar. Add the eggs one at a time, beating well after each addition. Add the flour and the lemon and vanilla extracts. Beat well. Gently fold in the 7-Up ¼ cup at a time. Pour the batter into the prepared pan. Bake for 1¼ to 1½ hours, or until a toothpick inserted in the middle of the cake comes out clean. Transfer the cake from the oven to a wire rack. Let it cool in the pan for 15 minutes. Unmold the cake onto the wire rack to cool completely. Transfer to a serving platter and dust with confectioners' sugar.

Makes one 10-inch tube cake

Left to right: Aint Marjell, her son, Larry, her husband, Uncle Joe Willie, late 1940s.

Aint Luverta's
DR PEPPER CAKE

Not only was Aint Luverta—my daddy's ainty—an excellent cook, she was also a tall and good-looking woman. She had everything—cream-colored skin and a head full of long, wavy hair—necessary (for the times) to be considered a beautiful "colored" woman. When I was a child, good hair was hair that was naturally thick and glossy, hair that didn't require lots of grease or a straightening comb to manage. Real good hair was hair that was straight, long, and bouncy, hair that was similar in texture to white folks' hair. If a woman had cream-colored skin and real good hair, she was considered the cream of the crop and was treated like royalty. Mama, who was cream-colored and had long, so-called "good" hair, disallowed the terms good hair *and* real good hair *in our house. She insisted that all hair was good hair, no matter how kinky or nappy it was.*

When rumor of this recipe first surfaced in our family, I expected the cake, with its Dr Pepper frosting, to taste like a drink of my favorite soda. But it didn't. The frosting reminds me of a piece of caramel candy.

Cake

2 cups all-purpose flour, sifted

1 teaspoon baking soda

2 cups granulated sugar

1 cup (2 sticks) unsalted butter

1½ cups miniature marsh-
   mallows

3 tablespoons unsweetened
   cocoa powder

1 cup Dr Pepper

2 eggs

1½ cups buttermilk

1 teaspoon vanilla extract

Dr Pepper Frosting

½ cup (1 stick) unsalted butter,
   softened

6 tablespoons Dr Pepper

3 tablespoons unsweetened
   cocoa powder

1 (1-pound) box confectioners'
   sugar, sifted

1 teaspoon vanilla extract

1 cup chopped pecans

Preheat the oven to 350°F.

Grease, but do not flour, a 9 by 13-inch pan. Set it aside.

To make the cake, in a large bowl, sift together the flour and baking soda. Gradually stir in the sugar. Set aside. In a saucepan, heat the butter, marshmallows, cocoa, and Dr Pepper. Stir constantly until the butter and the marshmallows are melted. Do not allow the mixture to boil. Pour the marshmallow mixture over the flour mixture. Beat well. Set aside. In another bowl, beat the eggs until they are light and fluffy. Stir in the buttermilk and vanilla extract. Mix well. Beat the egg mixture into the flour mixture until well blended and the batter is smooth. Pour the batter into the prepared pan. Bake for 50 to 55 minutes, or until the center of cake springs back when lightly touched. Let the cake cool on a rack for 10 minutes.

To make the frosting, in a saucepan, combine the butter, Dr Pepper, and cocoa powder. Bring the mixture to a boil over low heat, stirring constantly. Remove the pan from the heat. Gradually stir in the confectioners' sugar until the mixture is smooth, then fold in the vanilla extract and the pecans. Spread over the warm cake.

Make one 9 by 13-inch cake

Sister Baby's
WHISKEY CAKE

Sister Baby was Mama's second cousin. As sweet as she was, she was one of those girls who just wouldn't do right. If her mama, Cud'n Rachel, told her to be in by midnight, Sister Baby was gonna come in at one. If Cud'n Rachel warned her about a certain young man, that young man was the one Sister was gonna run around with. They say that if Cud'n Rachel hadn't spared the rod on Sister's rear end when she was a kid, things would have been much better for them both. But, Sister Baby was one of those "change-of-life" babies, and Cud'n Rachel was just too crazy about her to whip her little behind. By the time Sister Baby turned thirty, Mama said she looked weary and worn out, the result of bad men and fast living.

This is a very good cake; it's moist and not too heavy. The rich flavor of bourbon gives it its kick. Cooking good was about the only good thing that Sister Baby patterned after Cud'n Rachel.

---

1 cup raisins

1 cup bourbon or scotch

2 cups chopped pecans

2½ cups all-purpose flour

2 teaspoons ground cinnamon

1 teaspoon baking powder

¼ teaspoon baking soda

¼ teaspoon salt

1⅔ cups firmly packed light brown sugar

¾ cups (1½ sticks) unsalted butter, softened

5 eggs

Preheat the oven to 325°F.

Lightly grease and lightly flour a 9-inch square baking pan. Set it aside.

In a bowl, soak the raisins in the bourbon for 1 hour, then drain well, reserving both the raisins and the bourbon. In another bowl, toss the drained raisins and pecans with ½ cup of the flour. Coat well. In another bowl, stir together the remaining 2 cups of flour, cinnamon, baking powder, baking soda, and salt. Set the bowl aside. In a large bowl, cream the brown sugar and butter until light and fluffy, scraping the sides of the bowl often. Add the eggs one at a time, beating well after each addition. With a wooden spoon, stir one-third of the flour mixture, then add ½ cup of the bourbon, into the brown sugar and butter mixture. Repeat, then stir in the remaining flour mixture. Fold in the raisin and nut mixture. Spread the batter evenly into the prepared pan. Bake for 1½ hours, or until a toothpick inserted in the middle of the cake comes out clean. Transfer the cake from the oven to a wire cake rack. Let the cake stand in the pan on the rack for 10 minutes, then unmold the cake onto a wire cake rack to cool an additional 10 minutes. Transfer to a pretty cake plate, then brush the remaining ½ cup bourbon over the cake while it is still warm.

Note: During the holidays, after my grandmother took the cake out of the oven she would brush it with bourbon while it was still warm, then she'd cover the top of the cake with a bourbon-soaked swath of cheesecloth. Next, she'd cover the baking dish with foil or plastic wrap and refrigerate the cake for 48 hours, until it "ripened."

Makes one 9-inch cake

Sister Baby and one of her many admirers.

Miss Drucilla's
LEMON RUM CAKE

Miss Drucilla was My My's childhood best friend. Although Miss Drucilla never moved away from their native Mississippi community—Springfield—she and My My remained best friends their entire lives. Once a year Miss Drucilla traveled from Mississippi by bus to visit with My My in Michigan. It was an especially grueling trip for her because she weighed well over 400 pounds. By the time she'd reach My My, her feet were so swollen that we children had to take turns carrying Pop's silver tub, splishing and splashing with hot water and Epsom salts, to her bedside. While I wasn't fond of rubbing Miss Drucilla's soggy, swollen feet, I was fond of the way she was able to recollect events that made my grandmother giggle like a schoolgirl. I especially enjoyed listening to her and My My's reminiscences about Professor Green, their beloved country teacher. I loved hearing them marvel over his wisdom and intelligence. They attributed most of what they knew to him. Incidentally, their beloved, scholarly Professor Green had gone no further than the eighth grade. I guess to My My and Miss Drucilla that was quite an accomplishment, considering they'd only gone as far as the third.

When Miss Drucilla called to let us know that she was preparing for her yearly visit, My My would ask, "You got a taste for anything special, 'Cill? I'm gonna make my groceries this evenin'." Miss Drucilla's reply was always, "If it ain't too much trouble, I'd sho' like for you to fix me one of your lemon rum cakes . . . you know, the recipe that I give you."

Miss Drucilla's rum cake tastes especially good following a down-home seafood dinner.

Cake

6 tablespoons (¾ stick) unsalted butter, softened

¾ cup granulated sugar

3 eggs, separated

½ teaspoon grated lemon zest

½ teaspoon vanilla extract

¾ cup plain yogurt

3 tablespoons rum

1 cup cake flour, sifted

2 teaspoons baking powder

½ teaspoon salt

¼ teaspoon almond extract

¼ cup chopped almonds

Caramel Wine Syrup

½ cup dry red wine

¾ cups firmly packed brown sugar

¼ teaspoon ground cinnamon

Pinch of ground cloves

½ teaspoon vanilla extract

1 tablespoon unsalted butter

Preheat the oven to 350°F.

Lightly grease and flour a 10-inch tube pan. Set it aside.

To make the cake, in a bowl, cream the butter, sugar, egg yolks, lemon zest, and vanilla extract until fluffy. Set it aside. In a small bowl, combine the yogurt and rum. Mix well and set it aside. In another bowl, sift together the flour, baking powder, and salt. Alternate adding the flour mixture and the yogurt mixture to the butter mixture. Beat well after each addition. Beat for 1 minute more, until the mixture is light in texture. Combine the almond extract with the egg whites in a large bowl; beat the egg whites until they are stiff but not dry. Fold the egg whites gently into the cake batter along with the almonds. Pour the batter into the prepared pan. Bake for about 30 minutes, or until a toothpick inserted in the middle of the cake comes out clean. Transfer the cake from the oven to a wire rack. Let it cool in its pan for 15 minutes, then unmold the cake onto the wire rack to cool completely. Transfer to a serving platter.

To make the syrup, combine the wine, brown sugar, cinnamon, cloves, vanilla extract, and butter in a saucepan. Cook the mixture over low heat, stirring constantly, for 5 minutes, or until the spices are dissolved in the wine. Pour the syrup over the cake. Let the cake stand for 1 hour before serving.

Makes one 10-inch tube cake

Left to right: My cousin Freddy, me, my cousin Larry. My fourth birthday party included a homemade cake from Mama.

Miss LaLou's
OLD-TIME CHOCOLATE PUDDIN' RUM CAKE

Miss LaLou lived across the street from my grandmother. She was one of the most colorful persons in the neighborhood; at fifty-something, she was a genuine flirt. This rich and moist cake of Miss LaLou's was one of our favorites, even though us kids could have no more than a sliver because of its alcohol content. This is definitely a grown-up indulgence, not one for the kids. Occasionally, though, My My, who was extremely soft-hearted when it came to her "grands" (that's what she called us), would pretend to forget about the rum in the cake and cut us heaping slices.

Cake

½ cup chopped pecans

1 (18.5-ounce) box chocolate cake mix (without pudding)

1 (3-ounce) box instant chocolate pudding mix

4 eggs

½ cup vegetable oil

½ cup water

½ cup white rum

Rum Glaze

½ cup (1 stick) unsalted butter

1 cup granulated sugar

¼ cup white rum

¼ cup water

Preheat the oven to 350°F.

Place the pecans in the bottom of a greased 10-inch tube pan. Set it aside.

To make the cake, in a large bowl combine the cake mix, pudding mix, eggs, oil, water, and rum. Mix with an electric mixer on high speed for 2 minutes. Pour the batter into the prepared pan. Bake for 50 to 60 minutes, or until a toothpick inserted into the middle of the cake comes out clean. Let the cake stand in the pan for 30 minutes, then transfer it to a serving platter.

While the cake is cooling, start making the rum glaze. The glaze should be ready as soon as the cake is transferred to a serving platter.

To make the glaze, in a saucepan, cream together the butter, sugar, rum, and water. Stir well. Bring the mixture to a boil over medium heat and cook for 2 minutes. Remove the saucepan from the heat. Pour the glaze over the cake immediately.

Makes one 10-inch tube cake

  Sweets

My My's brother Rance during World War II.

Daddy and me before a Sunday drive, early 1960s.

Pies & Cobblers

Family reunion, Mississippi, late 1940s.

*W*hen I was a little girl, Mama's best friend, an older woman named Miss Ruthie, invited me and Mama to pick pears in the backyard of her young nephew, Rocky, and his wife, Loretta. I remember the day as if it were yesterday. It was warm and balmy; a gentle breeze meandered through the small fruit-tree grove in the couple's backyard. I especially remember the way the sunlight shone through the pear trees and the white picket fence that enclosed their well-manicured yard; it made pretty designs on the grass. Miss Ruthie's nephew and niece were the epitome of what I wanted to be and have when I grew up. Rocky was handsome and Loretta was pretty. Their little gingerbread house, complete with blue gingham curtains at the kitchen window, had the charm of something you'd see in a book of fairy tales. From an early age, I was a hopeless romantic, a dreamy little girl who thought blue gingham curtains, white picket fences, and a good-looking man and a pretty woman were the only ingredients necessary for lasting love and happiness. When Rocky and Loretta divorced a few years later, I was heartsick.

When I was little, someone was always giving Mama a bushel of this or a barrel of that. I hated it because that meant work—time away from play. Now I know that some of the closest moments between Mama and me happened in the kitchen while we were paring apples or peaches or pears to be canned and later put into pies or cobblers. I can see Mama now, sitting at the kitchen table, her legs spread wide apart, an old apron drooping between them, and a big plastic pail sitting on the floor to catch the peels. It was during those times when the two of us were home alone, paring apples or peaches or pears, that Mama tried her best to steer me away from the false notions that I had about love and marriage. Mama and my aunts were the kind of women who were not afraid to tell their little girls the truth about men and relationships—unlike the previous generation of grannies and aunties, who had sent the girls out of the room when the subject of men and love came up, fearing that if they heard such conversations they would become "womanish" way too soon. There wasn't much that my mother and aunts—even My My—wouldn't discuss in front of us in an attempt to prepare us for the art of womanhood.

Pies and cobblers were as much a part of my childhood as were pigtails and brightly colored barrettes and ribbons, and learning how to be a woman. Mama used to say, "There are three things that every black woman ought to know how to do well, and they are: make a good pan of corn bread, fry up a delicious batch of chicken, and make a tasty pie or cobbler."

Aint Helen and me, 1960s. My mother's sisters made me feel so special when I was a little girl.

BASIC PIE CRUST

Mama used to say, "A lot of folks don't know it, but the secret of a good pie is in the crust. You can't have a good pie if you don't have a good crust."

This recipe was given to Mama years ago by an older woman named Mrs. Falls. Mama, who was on her way to market that day, took a shortcut. She said she walked past Mrs. Falls's porch and said hello (in those days it was a shame to walk past a porch without speaking, even if you didn't know the people sitting on it). Mama said that somehow the two of them got to talking about pie crusts and Mrs. Falls invited her inside to sample the crust of an apple pie that she'd just made. Mama said it was the best crust she'd ever tasted. Mama and Mrs. Falls, who turned out to be an incredible baker, got to exchanging recipes and laughing, so Mama never did make it to the market that day.

This recipe makes a single 8- or 9-inch crust. Instructions for a double pie crust follow.

1⅓ cups all-purpose flour, sifted

½ teaspoon salt

½ cup vegetable shortening, chilled

1 egg, beaten

2 to 3 tablespoons cold milk, or more as needed

In a bowl, combine the flour and salt. Cut the shortening into the dry ingredients with a fork or by pinching the shortening into the flour mixture with your fingers. The result should be coarse crumbs and small clumps the size of peas. Add the egg and mix well. Add the milk 1 tablespoon at a time. Don't be afraid to add more milk if necessary to achieve a dough that's wet enough to form into a ball. Being careful not to overwork the dough, form the dough into a ball with your hands. Wrap the ball in plastic, then chill in the refrigerator for 30 minutes. Transfer the dough from the refrigerator to a lightly floured surface. Flatten the ball slightly and dust the top of it with flour before rolling it out with a rolling pin. Begin rolling at the center of the dough and work outward. Roll the dough out into a circle about 4 inches wider than the pie pan it will be placed in.

Double Pie Crust

2 cups all-purpose flour, sifted

½ teaspoon salt

1 cup vegetable shortening, chilled

1 egg, beaten

6 tablespoons cold milk

Follow the recipe instructions for the single pie crust. Divide the dough into 2 portions before rolling.

Mama's
SWEET POTATO PIE

In our family, every woman has her rendition of this delicious classic. Mama's version is my favorite.

3 large sweet potatoes

1 unbaked 9-inch pie crust
(page 57)

½ cup (1 stick) unsalted butter,
melted

½ cup dark corn syrup

1½ cups granulated sugar

2 eggs, beaten

½ cup buttermilk

½ teaspoon ground nutmeg

½ teaspoon ground cinnamon

½ teaspoon ground allspice

1 teaspoon vanilla extract

Pinch of salt

Whipped cream, for garnish

Wash the whole sweet potatoes and drain them. Place the sweet potatoes in a large pot and add cold water to cover by 2 inches. Bring the water to a boil over medium heat, and cook until the potatoes are tender, 30 to 40 minutes. (A fork should pierce the potatoes easily but they should not fall apart.) When the potatoes are done, drain and cool them.

Preheat the oven to 375°F. Prepare the pastry for a 9-inch single-crust pie. Set it aside.

When the potatoes are cool enough to handle, peel and mash them in the large bowl of an electric mixer. Add the melted butter, corn syrup, and sugar. Beat on medium speed. Discard the long, stringy fibers that collect around the electric beaters as you beat the filling. In the end, you want a smooth, string-free filling. Add the eggs one at a time. Beat well after each addition. Pour in the buttermilk. Add the nutmeg, cinnamon, allspice, vanilla extract, and salt. Beat until the filling is smooth. Pour the filling into the prepared pie crust. Bake for 35 to 40 minutes, or until a toothpick inserted into the center comes out clean. Remove from the oven and cool completely on a wire rack. Garnish with whipped cream.

Makes one 9-inch pie

Cud'n Ebelle's
OLD-FASHIONED SUGAR PIE

Cud'n Ebelle—My My's first cousin—worked for a rich white family in Mississippi. This family, who owned a furniture store in town, had a little girl who was the same age as Mama. Cud'n Ebelle, who was childless, made no attempt to hide the fact that Mama was her favorite. When the rich little girl got bored with dressing her Shirley Temple doll in the same doll clothes, she'd bag the used clothes and give them to Cud'n Ebelle with the directive, "Give these to your favorite little cousin, Ruth." The only doll Mama ever owned was a Topsy doll, with three pigtails, deep-dark skin, and bright ruby lips. Mama used to say with a chuckle that thanks to the pampered rich girl and Cud'n Ebelle's favoritism for her, Francis— Mama's Topsy doll—was the best-dressed colored doll in the state of Mississippi.

When we took trips to Mississippi to visit our relatives, Cud'n Ebelle would make us the most fabulous dinners (of course she set aside the biggest and the best pieces of the meal for Mama). This pie was always our favorite of her desserts. Although there are many versions of sugar pie, Cud'n Ebelle's is different because it calls for both granulated and brown sugar, and because it contains cinnamon and nutmeg.

---

1 unbaked 9-inch pie crust
   (page 57)

1 cup granulated sugar

1 cup firmly packed brown
   sugar

4 tablespoons cornstarch

½ teaspoon ground cinnamon

¼ teaspoon salt

¼ teaspoon ground nutmeg

3 eggs

1 egg yolk

2 cups evaporated milk

3 tablespoons unsalted butter,
   softened

1½ teaspoons vanilla extract

Preheat the oven to 350°F.

Prepare the pastry for a 9-inch single-crust pie. Set it aside.

In a large saucepan, combine the granulated and brown sugars, cornstarch, cinnamon, salt, and nutmeg. Mix well. Add the eggs and yolk one at a time, mixing well after each addition. Gradually stir in the milk until well blended. Cook over medium heat, stirring constantly, until the filling is thick and bubbly. Remove from the heat. Stir in the butter and vanilla extract. Pour the filling into the prepared crust. Bake for 40 to 45 minutes, or until a toothpick inserted in the middle comes out clean. Remove from the oven and cool completely on a wire rack before serving.

Makes one 9-inch pie

Mama's OLD-TIME MAPLE SYRUP PIE

With no brothers or sisters at home to amuse me when I was growing up, I spent a lot of my time in the company of grown folks. Mama and Daddy saw to it that I was comfortable, but not spoiled the way some only children were. I was obligated to make my bed, to place my dirty laundry in the hamper, and to carry my dirty dishes to the kitchen sink. Mama said, "The world ain't gonna treat you special 'cause you're an only child, and neither am I."

Even though Mama and Daddy believed in order and discipline in our house, they always managed to leave room for spontaneous excitement. Sometimes, out of nowhere, Daddy would say, "Who wants ice cream?" He didn't have to ask twice. I was already on my way out the door. Mama was full of surprises, too. Sometimes her surprises came on rainy afternoons while I was sprawled out on the living room floor, playing with my paper dolls. Suddenly, I'd get a whiff of something wafting from the kitchen that was so sweet and spicy that the aroma broke my concentration. I would lay my trinkets down and go to the kitchen door. "What you makin', Mama?" Acting like it wasn't a big deal, Mama would say, "Just a little maple pie, that's all."

I like this pie very much. It's simple, it's delicious, it's comfort food, it's love on a plate. When I make it, I like to serve each slice with a dollop of vanilla ice cream.

---

1 unbaked 9-inch pie crust (page 57)

2¼ cups maple syrup

¾ cup half-and-half

¼ cup all-purpose flour

4 eggs

1 cup chopped walnuts

Preheat the oven to 375°F.

Prepare the pastry for a 9-inch single-crust pie. Set it aside.

Combine the maple syrup, half-and-half, and flour in a large bowl; whisk until well blended. Add the eggs one at a time, blending well after each addition. Stir in the walnuts until they are well coated. Pour the filling into the prepared pie crust. Bake for 10 minutes, then decrease the heat to 350°F and bake for 30 to 35 minutes longer, or until the filling is set. Remove from the oven and cool on a wire rack for 30 minutes before serving.

Makes one 9-inch pie

Grammaw Mariah's
DEEP-DISH APPLE PIE

Nobody knew exactly how old Grammaw Mariah was; in fact, she didn't even know herself. She had clear memories of being separated from her mother when she was a little girl and memories of carrying water to the slaves on the plantation on which she lived. She was estimated to be well over a hundred when Mama and her sisters were little girls growing up in the South.

Grammaw, who was Pop's maternal grandmother, lived with Pop and My My before they came North. Even though Grammaw Mariah was more than a hundred years old, she still hadn't lost her desire for a man. They say that Mr. Murray Hickenbottom, who was still quite the ladies' man at the ripe old age of ninety-something, was forever disappointing Grammaw. At least once a month he'd propose to Grammaw, she'd accept, and my mother and her sisters—who were little girls—would dress Grammaw up real fine, replete with lacy things and white talcum powder on her face (Grammaw was as dark as midnight). Mama and her sisters would sit in the front yard with Grammaw, waiting for Mr. Hickenbottom to come so the two of them could walk to the courthouse in town. Of course old man Hickenbottom—the scoundrel—never came. Grammaw would sit out front in her lacy stuff 'til late afternoon, at which time she'd tell the girls, "We might's well go'n inside and commence to fixin' supper. Look like old man Hick's runnin' late." It was unfortunate for Mr. Murray Hickenbottom that he never married Grammaw, 'cause Grammaw Mariah may not have known how old she was, but she sure knew how to cook.

I like to combine a pinch of granulated sugar and a pinch of cinnamon and sprinkle it over the pie crust before I put it in the oven. This adds additional flavor and flair.

Deep-Dish Pie Crust

4½ cups all-purpose flour

1 teaspoon salt

1½ cups vegetable shortening, chilled

2 eggs, beaten

6 tablespoons cold milk

Apple Filling

9 to 12 baking apples, peeled, cored, and sliced

1 cup granulated sugar, plus more for sprinkling

½ cup firmly packed brown sugar

¼ teaspoon salt

½ teaspoon ground cinnamon

½ teaspoon ground nutmeg

⅛ teaspoon ground cloves

2 teaspoons vanilla extract

¼ cup (½ stick) unsalted butter, cut into small squares

1 egg, beaten

Preheat the oven to 450°F.

To make the pie crust, in a large bowl, combine the flour and salt. Cut the shortening into the dry ingredients with a fork or by pinching the shortening into the flour mixture with your fingers. The result should be coarse crumbs and small clumps the size of peas. Add the eggs and mix well. Add the milk 1 tablespoon at a time. Don't be afraid to add more milk if necessary to achieve a dough that's wet enough to form into a ball. Being careful not to overwork the dough, form the dough into a ball with your hands. Wrap the ball in plastic, then chill in the refrigerator for 30 minutes. Transfer the dough to a lightly floured surface and divide the dough into 2 portions. The portion for the bottom of the pan should be larger since it has more space to cover. Flatten the balls slightly and dust the top with flour before rolling out with a rolling pin. Begin rolling at the center of the dough and work outward. Roll the dough into 2 rectangles about 3 inches wider than the pan they will be placed in.

Line the bottom of a 9 by 13-inch rectangular glass baking dish dish with the bottom crust. In a large bowl, combine the apples and granulated and brown sugars. Mix well. Add the salt, cinnamon, nutmeg, cloves, and vanilla extract. Mix well. Pour the apple filling into the bottom pie crust. Dot with squares of butter. Place the top crust on top of the filling. Trim and crimp the edges to seal the crust; cut slits in the top. Lightly brush the top of the pie with the beaten egg, then sprinkle on a little sugar. Bake for 15 minutes. Decrease the heat to 350°F and cook for 45 minutes longer, or until the crust is golden brown and the juices are bubbling. If the edges of the crust brown too quickly, cover them with aluminum foil. Remove from the oven and cool on a wire rack. Serve warm or cold.

Note: I've heard people say that tart apples make the best apple pies, but I beg to differ; I've always preferred Golden Delicious. They're sweet, mellow, and richly flavored. They also hold up well when baked.

Makes one 9 by 13-inch pie

Me, age three, with a neighborhood boy. I've always been a hopeless romantic.

Aint Sis's

EGG PIE

Aint Sis was Big Mama's baby sister, but she wasn't anything like Big Mama. They say Aint Sis looked a lot like Dorothy Dandridge. She was a tall, light-skinned woman who wasn't well liked by the women in Springfield. She was good-looking and she knew it; she was the kind of woman who would grin in your face, then steal your man no sooner than you turned your back.

Big Mama used to say that the women in Springfield just didn't understand poor Sis. She said if the truth be told, Aint Sis wasn't stuttin' half of the men she stole. She said more than anything, Aint Sis stole people's boyfriends and husbands for the attention her ruthless shenanigans attracted. Big Mama said Aint Sis was one of those people who thrive on attention, 'cause without it, they feel overlooked. Big Mama said, "She been that way all her life. Even when she was a baby, Sis wasn't happy less'n somebody was standing 'round, making a fuss over her."

Aint Sis may have been a wanton hussy in the community, but in the kitchen she was an angel. Her cooking was divine. Everybody loved her egg pie.

---

1 unbaked 9-inch pie crust (page 57)

¼ cup (½ stick) unsalted butter, melted

1 cup granulated sugar

4 eggs

2½ cups evaporated milk

1 teaspoon cornstarch

Pinch of salt

1 teaspoon vanilla extract

Ground nutmeg, to taste

Preheat the oven to 425°F.

Prepare the pastry for a 9-inch single-crust pie. Set it aside.

In a large bowl, cream the butter and sugar together for 5 minutes. Beat in the eggs one at a time, beating well after each addition. Beat until the mixture is thick and lemon-colored. Add the milk, cornstarch, salt, and vanilla extract and mix well. Pour the filling into the prepared crust. Sprinkle the top of the pie with nutmeg to suit your taste. Bake for 15 minutes, then decrease the heat to 325°F and bake for 30 minutes, or until a toothpick inserted in the middle comes out clean. Remove from the oven and cool completely on a wire rack.

Note: To keep the bottom crust from getting soggy, I brush it with a little egg white and then chill the crust for about 20 minutes before filling it.

Makes one 9-inch pie

Miss Cora Belle's
FRIED FRUIT PIES

When I was a child, it was such a treat to come home from school and find a platter of fried hand pies cooling on the counter. Miss Cora Belle's recipe was the best.

Pastry

4 cups all-purpose flour, sifted

1 teaspoon salt

¼ cup granulated sugar

1 teaspoon baking soda

½ cup vegetable shortening

1¼ cups buttermilk

1 egg, beaten well

Filling

3 cups dried apples, peaches, or apricots

½ cup granulated sugar

¼ teaspoon ground allspice

1½ cups water, or more as needed

Confectioners' sugar, for sprinkling

Vegetable oil, for deep-frying

To make the pastry, in a large bowl, combine the flour, salt, sugar, and baking soda. Cut in the shortening with a fork or a pastry blender until the mixture is crumbly. Add the buttermilk and the egg. Mix lightly until all of the ingredients are well combined. Form the dough into a ball. Wrap the ball in plastic and refrigerate for at least 1 hour.

To make the filling, place the dried fruit, sugar, and allspice in a large, heavy saucepan. Add the water. Cover the pan and simmer over low heat until the fruit practically falls apart, about 20 minutes. The filling should be very tender, the consistency of thick preserves. Add more water if necessary to prevent scorching and to achieve the desired consistency. Remove the lid and continue cooking until all of the water evaporates.

To assemble the pies, remove the dough from the refrigerator after an hour. On a lightly floured surface roll out the dough to the thickness of pie crust. Cut the dough into circles 4 to 6 inches in diameter. Place a generous tablespoon of filling on one side of each circle. Fold the other side over the filling, then, using a fork, seal along the edges firmly. In a deep, heavy skillet, heat ½ inch of vegetable oil over medium heat. Deep-fry the pies, a few at a time, in the hot oil, turning once. When the pastries are golden brown, remove them from the skillet and drain on paper towels. Lightly sprinkle the pies with confectioners' sugar while the pies are still hot. Serve warm or cold.

Makes about 12 hand pies

Miss Ruthie's
OLD-FASHIONED PEACH COBBLER

Mama used to say, "Every woman should have an older woman friend and a younger one; the older woman friend to learn from and to lean on when you need a mature shoulder, the younger friend to keep you from gettin' too old too soon." Miss Ruthie was Mama's older friend. And despite the fact that she cooked "down-home," she wasn't really from down home. Miss Ruthie was born in Toronto, Canada. I always thought of her as an elegant woman. The china and silverware that most folks would've saved for company, Miss Ruthie used every day. She said she did so because she'd watched her mother save her good stuff for company; then, a few weeks after her mother's death, she watched her daddy's new wife inherit her mama's things, some of them with the tags still attached.

Peach cobbler is truly a down-home comfort dessert. Most peach cobbler recipes call for a double crust, but the bottom crust is not used to line the pie plate the way most bottom crusts are. The bottom crust becomes part of the filling, like a dumpling. Everyone who tasted Miss Ruthie's peach cobbler said it was the best they'd ever tasted.

---

1 unbaked double pie crust (page 57)

8 cups peeled and sliced fresh peaches

2 cups granulated sugar

¼ cup all-purpose flour

½ teaspoon ground cinnamon

½ teaspoon ground nutmeg

⅛ teaspoon ground allspice

½ cup (1 stick) unsalted butter, melted

1 teaspoon vanilla extract

Preheat the oven to 475°F.

Lightly butter an 8-inch square glass dish. Set it aside.

Prepare the pastry for a double-crust pie. Set it aside.

Combine the peaches, sugar, flour, cinnamon, nutmeg, and allspice in a 4-quart Dutch oven. Allow the mixture to sit until the dry ingredients are dissolved and a syrup forms, about 15 minutes. Bring the peach mixture to a boil over medium heat. Decrease the heat to low and cook until the peaches are tender, about 10 minutes. Remove the mixture from the heat and add the butter.

Roll out half of the pie pastry, then cut it into an 8-inch square. Spoon half of the peach mixture into the prepared dish. Cover the mixture with the pastry square. Bake 12 to 14 minutes, or until lightly browned. Take the dish out of the oven and spoon the remaining peach mixture over the baked pastry. Roll out the remaining pastry, then cut it into strips about an inch wide. Arrange the strips in a loose lattice pattern over the peach mixture. Bake an additional 15 to 20 minutes, or until browned. Remove from the oven. Serve warm.

Makes one 8-inch cobbler

  Sweets

Aint Pinky's
CANTALOUPE PIE

Aint Pinky was the baby sister of my grandfather Pop. She was as sweet and as feminine as her name suggests. They say Aint Pinky had a voice like Billie Holiday's. In the summertime, when the sun had gone down and folks were at their screens trying to catch a breeze, you could hear Aint Pinky through her kitchen window, cooking supper and moaning and groaning the words to a blues song that she made up as she went along.

When you want a change from the same old fruit pie, cantaloupe pie is a nice alternative. It's different, and it's delicious. Be sure to buy a ripe cantaloupe of good quality.

---

1 unbaked 9-inch pie crust
  (page 57)

Filling

1 large ripe cantaloupe

¾ cup granulated sugar

¼ cup all-purpose flour

3 egg yolks, beaten

2 tablespoons unsalted butter, melted

Meringue

3 egg whites

¼ teaspoon cream of tartar

6 tablespoons granulated sugar

Preheat the oven to 350°F.

Prepare the pastry for a 9-inch single-crust pie and pre-bake it for 10 to 12 minutes, until the crust is set. Set it aside.

To make the filling, cut the cantaloupe in half and scoop out the seeds and discard. Scoop the pulp into a large saucepan. Add half of the sugar and cook over medium heat until the melon is soft and tender, about 7 or 8 minutes. Using a fork, mash the melon as it cooks. In a large mixing bowl, combine the flour and the remaining sugar. Mix until well blended. Add the egg yolks and butter. Mix well. Add the mashed cantaloupe mixture to the egg yolk mixture. Mix well. Pour into the prebaked pie crust.

To make the meringue, in a large bowl, beat the reserved egg whites and cream of tartar together until frothy. Continue to beat the egg whites while gradually adding the 6 tablespoons sugar; beat until stiff peaks form. Cover the pie with the meringue and bake until the meringue is delicately browned, 12 to 15 minutes. Remove from the oven and cool for 30 minutes on a wire rack before serving.

Makes one 9-inch pie

Lillie Bea's
CHERRY COBBLER

Everybody knew it; Lillie Bea, a distant cousin to Mama, struggled in the kitchen. In a family that thought it was a disgrace when a woman couldn't cook, Lillie Bea stood out like a watermelon seed in a bowl of sugar. In our family of dedicated cooks, Lillie Bea was an oddity. While the other women in the family were either cooking or planning supper, Lillie Bea was somewhere looking in a mirror beautifying herself, rubbing scented oil into her cocoa-colored skin or painting her toenails bright red. They say Lillie Bea went to the beauty parlor every other morning, wore wide-brimmed hats and high-heeled pumps throughout the week, and paid Roosevelt, the stock boy at the A&P grocery store, a whole dollar just to tote her groceries one block to her house. Big Mama used to say, "Ain't nothin' worser'n a woman too cute to cook." This delicious cobbler is easy to fix. If it turned out for Cud'n Lillie Bea, it'll turn out for anybody.

½ cup (1 stick) unsalted butter

1 cup all-purpose flour

1 cup granulated sugar

1 teaspoon baking powder

1 cup milk

1 (21-ounce) can cherry pie filling

Preheat the oven to 275°F.

Place the butter in a 9 by 13-inch baking dish, then place the dish in the oven to melt the butter. Remove from the oven as soon as the butter is melted. In a bowl, combine the flour, sugar, and baking powder. Mix well. Stir in the milk. Pour the batter into the baking dish on top of the butter. Do not stir. Pour the cherry filling evenly on top of the batter. Do not stir. Increase the oven temperature to 350°F. Bake for 50 minutes, or until the cobbler is golden brown. Remove from the oven and cool on a wire rack for 20 to 30 minutes before serving.

Makes one 9 by 13-inch cobbler

Lillie Bea, early 1930s. Unlike the rest of the women in my family, Lillie Bea never took to the kitchen.

Aint Lula's
BUTTER BEAN PIE

Aint Lula was one of Pop's sisters. She was My My's favorite. She was the kind of sister-in-law who didn't automatically side with her brother; she stood for the truth, that's what My My used to say.

Of Pop's people, Aint Lula was my favorite, too. I liked her because she was feisty and articulate, a woman who didn't bite her tongue. Whatever she said about you behind your back, she would say to your face. They said Mama acquired her way with words from Aint Lula. Mama used to tell me, "Baby, there's power in the tongue. Learn as many words as you can, because the more words that you know, the better off you'll be. The words that come out of your mouth can either heal you or they can destroy you; they can move you forward, or they can keep you standin' still."

Not only was Aint Lula a fine in-law, she was also a fine cook. Her butter bean pies were a delight to savor. Their taste and aroma put you in the mind of sweet potato pies. This bean pie is unusual in that it calls for a cup of coconut.

---

1 unbaked 9-inch pie crust (page 57)

1 cup dried butter beans

3 cups water

2 cups granulated sugar

1 tablespoon all-purpose flour

½ cup (1 stick) unsalted butter, softened

1 tablespoon vanilla extract

1 cup sweetened flaked coconut

2 eggs, beaten

Pinch of salt

¼ teaspoon ground nutmeg

¼ teaspoon ground cloves

1 teaspoon half-and-half

Preheat the oven to 350°F.

Prepare the pastry for a 9-inch single-crust pie. Set it aside.

In a large pot, soak the beans in the water overnight. Drain the beans and remove the hulls. In a large pot, cover the beans with water and cook over medium heat until they are well done, 1 to 1½ hours. Check the beans occasionally to make sure they remain covered with the cooking liquid. If the tops of the beans become exposed during cooking, add very hot tap water to keep them covered. When the beans are tender, soft but not falling apart, remove the pot from the heat. Drain the beans in a colander. Pour the drained beans in a large bowl and mash with a fork. Add the sugar, flour, butter, vanilla extract, coconut, eggs, and salt to the mashed beans. Mix well. Add the nutmeg, cloves, and half-and-half. Blend together. Pour the bean filling into the prepared pie crust. Bake for 1 hour, or until a toothpick inserted in the middle comes out clean. Remove from the oven and cool completely on a wire rack before serving.

Note: You can leave the hulls on, but your pie won't be as attractive.

Makes one 9-inch pie

Aint Jessie Mae's
PECAN PIE

Aint Jessie Mae was married to Big Mama's brother, Sam. Aint Jessie's hobby was rummaging. She had an entire room devoted to her rummage sale finds. When I was a little girl, I'd say: "Aint Jessie, do you have a . . . ?" and whatever I was asking for, she usually had, buried in her rummage room.

Aint Jessie had four wild boys who had 'bout run her crazy, that's how Mama used to put it. She was constantly fidgeting and wringing her hands, she was so nervous. When we'd visit her, she couldn't sit still. She and Mama would be rapt in a good conversation, and then abruptly she'd get up and go into the kitchen. We could hear things falling on the floor, the clang of pots and pans, and the banging of the stove and the refrigerator door being slammed shut, but in a short while, we'd be called to the table to eat one of the best meals you'd ever want to taste. Aint Jessie Mae might've been a nervous wreck on account of her four wild boys, but she sure was an incredible cook.

Most times when I make this pie, the people who say "Just cut me a sliver" come back looking sheepish. "I'll have another little slice if you don't mind," they say. This luscious pecan pie does not call for white sugar. The thick corn syrup that the recipe calls for gives the pie a mild, sweet taste.

---

1 unbaked 9-inch pie crust (page 57)

1 cup light corn syrup

1 cup firmly packed dark brown sugar

½ cup (1 stick) unsalted butter, melted

Pinch of salt

1 teaspoon vanilla extract

3 eggs

1 heaping cup pecan halves

Preheat the oven to 350°F.

Prepare the pastry for a 9-inch single-crust pie. Set it aside.

In a large bowl, combine the corn syrup, brown sugar, butter, salt, and vanilla extract and mix well. In another bowl, lightly beat the eggs. Stir the eggs into the sugar mixture and mix well. Pour the filling into the prepared pie crust. Sprinkle the pecan halves on top of the filling. Bake for 45 to 50 minutes, or until the surface of the pie appears golden brown and slightly crusty. Remove from the oven and cool completely on a wire rack before serving.

> *Note:* It may be necessary to cover the edges of the pie crust with aluminum foil during the last 15 minutes of baking to prevent her crust from getting too brown.

Makes one 9-inch pie

A Taste of Down-Home
PEAR COBBLER

On cold winter days, this hearty down-home confection was enjoyed by our family. Served hot or cold, topped with whipped cream or vanilla ice cream, this cobbler tastes delightful.

3 fresh pears, peeled, cored, and sliced

2 cups granulated sugar

2 tablespoons unsalted butter, melted, plus ½ cup (1 stick) unsalted butter

Pinch of ground cinnamon, plus more for sprinkling

Pinch of ground nutmeg, plus more for sprinkling

1 tablespoon cornstarch

½ cup water

1 cup milk

1 cup all-purpose flour

2 teaspoons baking powder

Pinch of salt

Preheat the oven to 350°F.

In a large bowl, combine the pears with 1 cup of the sugar, the melted butter and the pinches of cinnamon and nutmeg. Set the bowl aside. In another bowl, dissolve the cornstarch in the water. Stir the cornstarch mixture into the pear mixture. In another bowl, combine the milk, the remaining 1 cup sugar, the flour, baking powder, and salt. Beat until the batter is smooth; the mixture will be thin. Place the butter in a 9 by 13-inch baking dish, then place the dish in the oven to melt the butter. Remove from the oven as soon as the butter is melted. Pour the batter over the melted butter. Spoon the pears over the batter. The pears should not extend more than 1 inch from the top of the dish. Sprinkle with additional cinnamon and nutmeg. Bake for 1 hour, or until a toothpick inserted in the middle comes out clean. Remove from the oven and serve hot or cold.

Makes one 9 by 13-inch cobbler

Left to right: Aint Sis, Aint Betty Jean, unidentified man. Rural Mississippi, early 1940s.

Aint Bessie's
PINEAPPLE PIE

Aint Bessie was married to My My's handsome and debonair baby brother, Rance. Uncle Rance owned two barber shops in Detroit. As a result of the nature of his business—people from all walks of life were constantly coming and going—Uncle Rance was well known in the city. He was well liked by the men and, unfortunately, just as well by the women. When I was a little girl, rumors concerning Uncle Rance and other women floated around our family; it made me feel sorry for Aint Bessie. In fact, all of the women in my family felt sorry for her. They loved her, and said there wasn't a sweeter, more kind-hearted woman. However, our pity for Aint Bessie dissipated after My My spent a long weekend in Detroit with her baby brother and his wife. When she got back, the first thing that came out of My My's mouth was, "Hmmp. There ain't nothing to feel sorry for Bessie about. She gets whatever she wants. And believe me, Rance ain't goin' nowhere." My My went to bragging about the assortment of minks in Aint Bessie's closet, about all of the diamond pieces in her jewelry box, about the thick porterhouse steaks Uncle Rance kept stacked inside the refrigerator, and about the way that wherever they went, Uncle Rance let the people know that nobody, absolutely nobody, meant more to him than his wife. My My said Aint Bessie came to life in Uncle Rance's absences. Said she'd fry up a big, juicy porterhouse, get on the phone and giggle with her girlfriends, model her minks in front of the mirror, and rearrange the diamonds on her fingers. My My said, "It takes a wise woman to understand that some men just have to complete their race in the streets before they're ready to come in. Bessie is a wise woman."

Not many people we knew had tasted pineapple pie until they'd tasted the ones our family used to make. One bite, and most people were hooked on them. Our pineapple pies soon became the dessert our friends, neighbors, and church members most requested when they invited us to things that required a dish to pass. My My used to say, "You have to give credit where credit is due: Bessie's pineapple pies are the best."

---

1 unbaked 9-inch pie crust (page 57)

1 cup granulated sugar

½ cup (1 stick) unsalted butter, melted

3 eggs, lightly beaten

2 tablespoons all-purpose flour

¼ teaspoon salt

½ teaspoon ground nutmeg

1 (20-ounce) can crushed pineapple, drained

½ cup evaporated milk

3 tablespoons sour cream

2 teaspoons vanilla extract

Preheat the oven to 350°F.

Prepare the pastry for a 9-inch single-crust pie. Set it aside.

In a bowl, cream together the sugar and butter. Add the eggs and mix well. In another bowl, combine the flour, salt, and nutmeg. Add to the sugar mixture and mix well. Stir in the drained pineapple, milk, sour cream, and vanilla extract. Pour the filling into the prepared pie crust. Bake for 45 minutes, or until the pie is lightly browned. Remove from the oven and cool on a wire rack. Serve warm or cold.

Makes one 9-inch pie

Make You Slap Yo' Mama
BLUEBERRY PIE

When My My talked about something that was exceptionally tasty, she would say, "Honey, it'll make you slap yo' mama, it's so good." When I was little, My My's statement baffled me. While I had sampled many good-tasting things in my life, I had never tasted anything that good.

When choosing berries for this pie, remember that it's true what they say: The blacker the berry, the sweeter the juice.

1 unbaked double pie crust
(page 57)

4 cups fresh blueberries

2 teaspoons fresh lemon juice

1½ cups granulated sugar

1 teaspoon grated lemon zest

¼ cup all-purpose flour

½ teaspoon ground cinnamon

2 tablespoons unsalted butter

Preheat the oven to 450°F.

Prepare the pastry for a double-crust pie. Line the bottom and the sides of a 9-inch pie pan with the bottom crust. Set it aside.

Place the blueberries in a large bowl. Sprinkle them with the lemon juice. In another bowl, combine the sugar, lemon zest, flour, and cinnamon. Sprinkle the sugar mixture on the blueberries. Toss the berries gently, until the flour mixture has been evenly distributed. Pour the blueberry mixture into the crust. Dot with the butter. Place the second crust on top of the filling, trim and fold the edges of the top crust under the edges of the bottom crust, then flute the edges and cut slits in several places on top of crust. Or, if you prefer, cut the remaining pie crust into ten ½-inch-wide strips and arrange the strips in a lattice pattern over the pie filling. Bake for about 10 minutes. Decrease the heat to 350°F and bake until the crust is light golden brown, about 30 to 40 minutes. Remove from the oven and cool completely on a wire rack before serving.

> *Note:* Blueberries have such a gorgeous deep-blue color that I think it's much nicer to display them under a pretty lattice top than to hide them under a dome of crust.

Makes one 9-inch pie

Cud'n Jerland's
LEMON MERINGUE PIE

Couldn't nobody outdo Cud'n Jerland when it came to making a lemon meringue pie. After many years of prodding, Cud'n Jerland finally confided that her secret was in the combination of cornstarch and flour that she used as a thickener. She said this accounted for her pie's creamy texture, as opposed to the slick texture of most lemon meringue pies.

---

1 baked 9-inch pie crust
   (page 57)

Filling

1½ cups granulated sugar

¼ cup cornstarch

3 tablespoons flour

¼ teaspoon salt

1½ cups water

3 egg yolks

3 tablespoons unsalted butter

2 teaspoons grated lemon zest

½ cup fresh lemon juice

Meringue

½ cup granulated sugar

1 tablespoon cornstarch

2 tablespoons cold water

½ cup boiling water

3 egg whites

Pinch of salt

1 teaspoon vanilla extract

Preheat the oven to 350°F.

Prepare the pastry for a 9-inch single-crust pie. Bake it in the oven for 10 to 12 minutes, or until the crust is set. Remove the crust from the oven and set it aside.

To make the filling, combine the sugar, cornstarch, flour, and salt in a large, heavy saucepan. Gradually whisk in the water. Cook over medium heat, whisking constantly, until the mixture thickens and comes to a boil. Continue to boil while stirring vigorously for 3 to 8 minutes, until it has a clear, uncloudy appearance. Remove the saucepan from the heat. Place the egg yolks in a bowl, then beat well with a fork. Gradually stir half of the sugar mixture into the egg yolks, whisking constantly. Pour the egg yolk mixture into the saucepan containing the sugar mixture. Bring to a boil again over medium heat. Decrease the temperature to low. Cook and stir 3 minutes, then remove from the heat. Stir in the butter, lemon zest, and lemon juice. Mix well. Pour the filling into the prebaked pie crust.

To make the meringue, blend 2 tablespoons of the sugar, the cornstarch, and cold water in a large saucepan. Stir until the cornstarch dissolves. Add the boiling water and cook over medium heat until the mixture is thick and clear. Cool completely. In a large bowl, beat the egg whites until they are foamy. Gradually beat in the remaining 6 tablespoons sugar, 1 tablespoon at a time. Add the salt and vanilla extract to the egg whites, and slowly beat in the cold cornstarch mixture. Beat at high speed for 2 to 3 minutes. Continue to beat until the whites form stiff and glossy peaks. Spread the meringue over the lemon filling to the edges of the pie crust, covering the filling completely. Bake for 10 to 15 minutes, or until the meringue is lightly browned. Remove from the oven and cool completely on a wire rack before serving.

Makes one 9-inch pie

Mama's cousin Jerland (center) made lemon meringue pies that were divine.

Cud'n Della's
WHITE POTATO PIE

Cud'n Della, My My's favorite first cousin, brought this delightful pie to all of our family gatherings. Once you taste this unique and delicious pie—it will put you in the mind of pumpkin pie, because it resembles it in taste and texture—you won't look at white potatoes quite the same.

1 unbaked 9-inch pie crust (page 57)

1 large russet potato, peeled, boiled, and mashed well

3 tablespoons unsalted butter

1 cup granulated sugar

2 eggs, separated

1 cup evaporated milk

Grated zest and juice of ½ lemon

Pinch of ground nutmeg

Preheat the oven to 350°F.

Prepare the pastry for a 9-inch single-crust pie. Set it aside.

To make the filling, combine the mashed potato, butter, and sugar in a large bowl. Blend until the mixture is smooth. In another bowl, beat the egg yolks. Add the egg yolks to the mashed potato mixture a little bit at a time, mixing well after each addition. Add the milk, lemon zest, and juice. Blend well. In another bowl, whip the egg whites until almost stiff, then, with a large spoon, fold the egg whites into the mashed potato mixture. Pour the filling into the prepared pie crust. Sprinkle nutmeg on top. Bake for 40 to 45 minutes, or until a toothpick inserted in the middle comes out clean. Remove from the oven and cool completely on a wire rack before serving.

Makes one 9-inch pie

Big Mama's
BUTTERMILK PIE

There was always a stern look on Big Mama's face, but it wasn't because she was ornery, it was because she kept her focus on the chores that needed to be done. Her house was spotless. During the day, as she cleaned house, she kept her teeth in a Mason jar on top of her dresser. Me and Cud'n Junior would sneak into her bedroom when she was out back hanging wash and we'd take turns wearing her teeth. Once, we got to playing so hard that we forgot to put Big Mama's teeth back in the jar. That evening, Brother Bartles—she'd deny it, but everyone said they were sweet on one another—stopped by, and when Big Mama ran to fetch her teeth she couldn't find them. She had to talk to Brother Bartles looking shame-faced, with one hand covering her mouth. They say that when Big Mama was young, she was an attractive woman, tall and shapely. As a kid, I would look at her and no matter how hard I tried, I couldn't imagine that anybody who kept her teeth in a Mason jar all day had ever been cute.

If you've never had buttermilk pie, you're in for a treat. You won't know you're eating buttermilk because Big Mama's recipe turns out a rich and sweet dessert that will satisfy any sweet tooth.

1 unbaked 9-inch pie crust
  (page 57)

1½ cups granulated sugar

3 tablespoons all-purpose flour

¼ teaspoon salt

1 teaspoon ground nutmeg

3 eggs

2 cups buttermilk

¼ cup (½ stick) unsalted
  butter, melted and cooled

1 tablespoon vanilla extract

Preheat the oven to 350°F.

Prepare the pastry for a 9-inch single-crust pie. Set it aside.

In a large bowl, combine the sugar, flour, salt, and nutmeg. Mix thoroughly. In another large bowl, beat the eggs. Add the buttermilk, butter, and vanilla extract to the beaten eggs. Gradually add the buttermilk mixture to the sugar mixture. Blend well. Pour the filling into the prepared pie crust and bake for 35 to 40 minutes, or until a toothpick inserted in the center comes out clean. Remove from the oven and cool completely on a wire rack before serving.

Makes one 9-inch pie

Miss Nellie's
LITTLE OF NOTHING PIE

Miss Nellie was an old white woman who stayed in the neighborhood long after all the other white folks moved away. She wore pastel-colored sweaters draped over flower-print dresses, thick beige-colored hose, and shiny old-lady comfort shoes that squished against the pavement when she walked. Miss Nellie lived a quiet and unimpressive life among her "colored" neighbors. If it weren't for the rumor that her pantry shelves were lined with hundreds of coffee cans stuffed with hundred-dollar bills, most people wouldn't have given Miss Nellie a second glance as she squished through the neighborhood.

When she was on her way to and from market, Miss Nellie would stop and chat with My My, or with whoever was sitting on the porch. She often talked about how hard times had been for her and her kinfolk in Kentucky during the Depression. She said her mama had to make meals out of what they had—a little of nothing. I remember the day she gave My My this recipe. I couldn't have been more than ten as I listened intently from behind the screen door while Miss Nellie talked about growing up on chitlins and pot liquor, "just like the coloreds." And how it had been a treat when her mama took the little that they had and made her little of nothing pie.

This eggless pie tastes good plain, but sometimes I sprinkle about half a cup of sweetened shredded coconut on top before I put it into the oven to give it a little flair.

---

1 unbaked 8-inch pie crust
   (page 57)

1½ cups milk

⅓ cup all-purpose flour

½ cup granulated sugar

1 teaspoon vanilla extract

2 tablespoons unsalted butter

Pinch of ground cinnamon

Preheat heat oven to 350°F.

Prepare the pastry for an 8-inch single-crust pie. Set it aside.

In a large bowl, combine the milk, flour, sugar, and vanilla extract. Mix thoroughly. Pour into the prepared crust. Dot with butter and sprinkle with cinnamon. Bake until a toothpick inserted in the middle comes out clean. Remove from the oven and cool completely on a wire rack before serving.

> *Note:* The original recipe calls for only 3 tablespoons of sugar, but My My used to say, "If you go'n put sugar in something, *put* sugar in it."

Makes one 8-inch pie

  Sweets

OLD-FASHIONED WALNUT-RAISIN PIE

This spicy delight is similar to mincemeat pie in taste and texture. In our family, raisin pie is a favorite of both the young and the old during the holidays.

1 unbaked 9-inch pie crust (page 57)

1 cup walnuts, chopped

1 cup seedless raisins

5 eggs

1 cup granulated sugar

½ cup firmly packed dark brown sugar

¾ teaspoon ground cinnamon

¾ teaspoon ground nutmeg

¾ teaspoon ground allspice

3 tablespoons fresh lemon juice

3 tablespoons milk

Preheat the oven to 350°F.

Prepare the pastry for a 9-inch single-crust pie.

Spread the walnuts and the raisins evenly on the bottom of the pie crust. Set the crust aside. In a large bowl, beat the eggs until they are frothy. Gradually beat the white and the brown sugars into the egg mixture. Add the cinnamon, nutmeg, and allspice. Blend well. Add the lemon juice and milk and mix well. Pour the mixture over the walnuts and raisins. Bake for 50 minutes, or until a toothpick inserted into the center comes out clean. Remove from the oven and cool completely on a wire rack before serving.

Makes one 9-inch pie

Pop's beagle hound Pal. Folks were always bringing My My some of their home cooking. If she didn't think they were clean enough, she would send the food back to Pal. Pal would eat anything. (In the background is Pal's sister, Lucy.)

As Good to Her Cooking As She Was to Herself

My My wasn't the kind of self-sacrificing women who would scrimp and pinch pennies, neglecting herself for the sake of her husband or her children. If the truth be told, she was quite the opposite. She loved jewelry, pretty church dresses, glossy patent leather shoes, and pillbox hats, like Jackie Kennedy wore. My My had two chiffoniers crammed full that proved she didn't neglect herself. She and Pop caught the bus to town nearly every Saturday morning, and after they'd paid up their accounts they went their separate ways, Pop to the hardware store, the paint store, and eventually a bench in the park, My My to Seitner's Dress Shop, Jacobson's Department Store, Granville's Shoe Store, and eventually the Hat Shop. When they'd meet up again, on the corner of East Genesee and Washington, the center of downtown, to commence their short walk home, My My would always have something new: fragrant toiletries that she'd bought at the five-and-dime, silk stockings for church the next day, a dress that she'd caught on sale, a new pillbox hat.

When they got home, My My would go straight to her bedroom, where we could hear her emptying out the contents of her bags. She would soon emerge, sporting her new perfume, her new dress, her new shoes, her new pillbox hat, her new *whatever*. She'd go to the mirror on her chiffonier in the family room, turn and twist to study her reflection, and then she'd come out and model for Pop. "How do I look? Is this too long? Too short? Too loose? Too tight? Do you like it? Or do you think I should take it back?" Most times, when she'd turn her back, Pop would look at us kids and hunch his shoulders and grimace, as if to say, "Women! Who understands them?" Behind his back, My My would tell us girls, "A man expects a woman to want pretty baubles and trinkets. Why disappoint him?"

When My My turned out one of her pies to cool, we all knew that we were in for a treat. We knew she hadn't scrimped on the quality of the ingredients because she was as good to her cooking as she was to herself. She prepared her sweet dishes with reverence; only the finest ingredients would do. The fruits, the berries, the sugar, and the nuts that went inside her pies were usually *brand name;* so were the eggs, the flour, and the shortening that formed the flaky crusts that encased them. When I was a little girl, I was glad that My My was the kind of woman who didn't neglect herself, because her regard for herself was also reflected in the things that she cooked.

Pop and My My relaxing on the loveseat in their family room, early 1960s.

Left to right: Pop, his sister Ida, and my cousin Larry. Illinois, 1960s.

Puddings & Desserts

My fourth birthday party.

*T*he women of my childhood did not have fancy college degrees, speak the King's English, belong to afternoon tea circles, or have the luxury of lying around while other women waxed their kitchen floors. They didn't carry expensive briefcases or rush off to business meetings. They didn't look to the business world, or, for that matter, to any world beyond their homes and communities to give them a sense of who they were as women. Without the financial ability to contribute blank checks to their favorite causes, they quietly went about the community building and nurturing, seeking God and helping those who were downtrodden. "He'll come back." "Have faith in God." "Not all good-bye's are forever." "If you need anything just let me know." Their words were the balm that healed the sick and the hurting.

Under the tutelage of my mother, my grandmother, my aunts, and other strong women with names like Big Mama, Miss Cora Belle, and Aint Sug, I came to understand that being a woman is powerful and magical, and has nothing to do with age or beauty. Many of the women who influenced me the most were neither young nor beautiful, neither educated nor worldly. I grew up watching these women keep immaculate houses, prepare delicious, robust meals, and tend to the sick, all the while operating out of a strong sense of their feminine worth, in particular their ability to give love, warmth, and nurturing. I saw these women quietly making their daily rounds—doing the dishes, making beds, hanging out the wash, ironing and folding the clothes, sweeping, cooking supper—and I witnessed something magical in the way they turned mundane chores into sacred rituals.

Like the women of my childhood, the puddings and the desserts they served were without a lot of dramatic flavorings and garnishes. Most of them were just plain old down-home confections that were served as they were, without contrived grandeur. In fact, most times, when someone put a meringue on top of a pudding or a dessert, that was as fancy as it got.

In our family, serving a pudding or a deep-dish dessert on a weekday was a way for the cook to share love and to nurture her family. Nothing gave a stressed spirit, young or old, more comfort than to walk into a house engulfed in the rich and buttery aroma of a luscious bread pudding cooling on the stove top, or to open the kitchen door onto the opulent fragrance of spices and berries mixing together in the juice of a berry pudding. The puddings and the desserts of my childhood were quick and easy to make. Once everybody in the house came together on what they had a taste for, nobody had to run to the store to buy anything. All of the ingredients were right in the kitchen: eggs, butter, sugar, rice, day-old bread, vanilla, and sweet milk. I think of the puddings and the desserts of my childhood as feel-good foods, foods that were comprised mainly of inexpensive ingredients but were rich in flavor, comfort, and love. And weekday healing.

My My's younger sister Bulah was truly a Renaissance woman of the 1930s and 1940s. She was college educated, an entepreneur, well traveled, and a staunch supporter of the advancement of women.

Aint Bulah's
DOWN-HOME BREAD PUDDIN'

This was Mama's favorite. She said there wasn't a soul who could make a better bread pudding than Aint Bulah. Not a soul. Aint Bulah said, "The secret's in the sauce."

Pudding

3½ cups evaporated milk (Aint Bulah wouldn't use anything other than Pet brand)

1 loaf day-old bread, broken into ½-inch pieces (see Note)

½ cup (1 stick) unsalted butter, softened

1½ cups granulated sugar

4 egg yolks, beaten

2 teaspoons vanilla extract

Pinch of salt

1 teaspoon ground cinnamon

1 teaspoon ground nutmeg

1 cup raisins

3 tablespoons rum

Rum Sauce

½ cup (1 stick) unsalted butter

1 cup water

2 tablespoons all-purpose flour

¾ cup granulated sugar

2 tablespoons rum

2 teaspoons vanilla extract

Preheat the oven to 350°F.

Generously grease a 2-quart casserole dish. Set it aside.

To make the pudding, heat the milk over low heat in a saucepan until it is hot, but not boiling. Remove from the heat and add the bread pieces. Let them stand in the milk until all of the milk is absorbed. The bread should be soft but not mushy. Add the rum to the raisins and set aside. In a large bowl, cream together the butter and sugar. Beat in the egg yolks, vanilla extract, salt, cinnamon, and nutmeg. Mix well. Add this mixture to the bread mixture. Stir well. Gently stir in the raisins. Pour the mixture into the prepared casserole dish. Bake for 1 hour, or until a toothpick inserted in the middle comes out clean. Remove from the oven.

To make the rum sauce, in a saucepan, bring the butter and water to a boil over medium heat. Add the flour and sugar, whisking constantly. Whisk in the rum and vanilla extract. Cook, stirring constantly, until the mixture bubbles. Remove the saucepan from the heat and serve hot over the warm or room-temperature pudding.

Note: Be sure to use a loaf of bread, not slices. Slices of bread will not result in a successful pudding.

Serves 4 to 6

Big Mama's
'NANA PUDDIN'

Big Mama said the key to a good banana pudding was in the bananas. She said the bananas had to be good and ripe: yellow, with brown specks on the peel.

Pudding

1½ cups granulated sugar

3 tablespoons flour

Pinch of salt

4 egg yolks

3 cups milk

¼ cup (½ stick) unsalted butter

1 teaspoon vanilla extract

1 (12-ounce) box vanilla wafers

4 to 5 large ripe bananas

Meringue

4 egg whites, at room
temperature

5 tablespoons granulated sugar

¼ teaspoon cream of tartar

½ teaspoon vanilla extract

Preheat the oven to 350°F.

Lightly grease the bottom of a 1½ quart casserole dish. Set it aside.

To make the pudding, combine the sugar, flour, and salt in a large saucepan. Mix the ingredients well, then set them aside. In a bowl, beat the egg yolks until they are smooth. Gradually add the milk to the yolks while continuing to beat. Pour the egg mixture into the sugar mixture. Combine thoroughly, then add the butter. Cook the pudding over low to medium heat until it thickens. Stir in the vanilla extract, then let the mixture cool. Line the bottom of the prepared casserole dish with a third of the vanilla wafers. Peel the bananas, then slice them into ¾-inch rounds. Place a third of the banana slices in a layer on top of the layer of wafers, then spread a third of the cooled custard on top. Continue layering the wafers, bananas, and custard until you have 3 layers of each ingredient, finishing with the custard. Let the pudding cool for 10 to 15 minutes before topping with meringue.

To make the meringue, in a large bowl beat the egg whites with an electric mixer until they form soft peaks. Add the sugar a tablespoon at a time, followed by the cream of tartar. Carefully fold in the vanilla extract. Spread the meringue over the cooled pudding. Bake for 12 to 15 minutes, or until the meringue is golden brown. Remove from the oven. Serve warm or chilled.

Note: You can cover and refrigerate leftovers, but be warned: While leftover banana pudding may still taste delicious, it's not a pretty sight. In other words, it doesn't hold up well.

Serves 4 to 6

Aint Sug's

PUNKIN' PUDDIN'

Despite the fact that Aint Sug—My My's ainty, Big Mama's sister—grew up in the country and main-tained one of the most beautiful flower and vegetable gardens you'd ever want to see, she was deathly afraid of creepy-crawly critters. Searching for an easier life, Aint Sug moved to Chicago in the early 1930s. Unfortunately, when she'd travel back home to visit, the folks down South would accuse her of having become uppity. They said that because Aint Sug had had a little taste of city life, she thought she had become too good for the country. They'd claim she was "putting on airs" when they'd hear her blood-curdling screams coming from her mother's garden—a mile away—each time an insect landed on her arm. The country folks couldn't understand how a woman born and raised in the country could be afraid of country critters. When the folks'd hear one of Aint Sug's earsplitting screams coming from the garden up the road, they'd roll their eyes and say, "There goes Sug, puttin' on airs again."

Big Mama used to say, "As sure as you're livin' in this world, there's gonna be times when you'll be misunderstood."

This sweet baked pumpkin pudding is irresistible. The crispy meringue topping will call you back for more.

Pudding

4 cups canned pumpkin

1½ cups granulated sugar

2 cups evaporated milk

3 egg yolks

3 rounded tablespoons all-purpose flour

2 teaspoons baking powder

½ teaspoon ground ginger

½ teaspoon ground cloves

½ teaspoon ground cinnamon

1 teaspoon vanilla extract

3 tablespoons unsalted butter, softened

Meringue

3 egg whites

¼ teaspoon cream of tartar

1 teaspoon vanilla extract

1 cup granulated sugar

Preheat the oven to 350°F.

Lightly grease a 9 by 13-inch baking pan. Set it aside.

To make the pudding, in a large bowl, combine the pumpkin, sugar, and milk. Mix until the ingredients are well combined and the pumpkin mixture is smooth. Add the egg yolks, flour, baking powder, ginger, cloves, cinnamon, and vanilla extract to the mixture. Mix well. Pour the pudding into the prepared pan. Dot with the butter. Bake for 30 to 45 minutes, or until a toothpick inserted in the middle comes out clean. Remove from the oven, but do not turn the oven off.

To make the meringue, in a large bowl, beat the egg whites, cream of tartar, and vanilla extract until soft peaks form. Gradually add the sugar while beating until stiff peaks form. Using your fingers, touch the meringue to make sure that some sugar grains can still be felt in the meringue. Spread the meringue on top of the cooked pudding that has just been removed from the oven, then return it to the oven and bake until the meringue is lightly browned, about 12 to 15 minutes. Turn the oven off and let the pudding stand inside the oven until the meringue is crisp. Remove it from the oven and serve hot.

Serves 4 to 6

Miss Cora Belle's
BLACKBERRY JAM PUDDIN'

This is good! During picking season, My My, Big Mama, and Miss Cora Belle, who lived on the other side of the picket fence in My My's backyard, would wrap their heads in thick, bleached-white scarves, slip into sturdy work jeans with rolled-up cuffs, and pile into Miss Cora's old Ford Woody station wagon and travel thirty-five miles to the blackberry farm in Fenton. My My and Big Mama canned jars of blackberry jam just to put into this pudding. They said they'd run across several blackberry pudding recipes, but they declared the one Miss Cora shared with them was the best.

1 cup granulated sugar

½ cup (1 stick) unsalted butter

2 eggs

1 cup blackberry jam

1 teaspoon vanilla extract

1 cup self-rising flour

1 teaspoon ground cinnamon

½ teaspoon ground nutmeg

Pinch of salt

¾ cup milk

1 cup chopped pecans

Whipped cream (optional)

Confectioner's sugar (optional)

Preheat the oven to 350°F.

Lightly grease a 2-quart baking dish. Set it aside.

In a large bowl, cream together the sugar, butter, and eggs. Add the jam and beat until the mixture is light. Stir in the vanilla extract. Add the flour, cinnamon, nutmeg, and salt. Mix well after each addition. Stir in the milk. Add the pecans and stir until they are evenly distributed. Pour the pudding into the prepared dish. Bake for 45 minutes, or until the top looks spongy. Serve warm with whipped cream or dusted with confectioner's sugar, if desired.

Serves 4 to 6

Sister Rose Johnston's
BREAD AND BUTTER PUDDIN'

Some women are bona fide church divas, real Sunday morning socialites, if you will. If you've spent any time in church you'll know exactly what I mean. Church divas easily make their presence known. They wear the widest-brimmed hats, the longest-sleeved gloves, and they have patent leather shoes and shiny pocketbooks to match everything. Church divas holler in the loudest spiritual tongues and they dance the Holy Ghost dance the longest. Church divas are the first ones knocking at your door with a dish to pass when your family suffers a misfortune, they belong to all of the church committees, they park their big cars next to the space reserved for the reverend, and they have a seat reserved on the front pew. Sometimes, even in death, church divas outshine the rest of us. When Rose Johnston—a real church diva—died, they displayed her in a bronze-colored casket that matched the gold-colored evening gown and the long-sleeved gloves that she wore. Her jet-black hair sparkled like patent leather and her nut-brown skin looked as supple as it had on the day she'd been born. They said she looked like she had just walked off the Ed Sullivan show; said she looked a lot like Mary Wilson of the Supremes. The first thing us kids wanted to know when My My walked in from the funeral was, "Did she have a big turnout? Did they send her off nice?" (Church divas are the subject of as much curiosity in death as they are in life.) According to My My, "Sister Johnston looked better laying in the casket than most of us looked sittin' in the pews."

This is a good, comforting dessert. Sister Johnston brought her bread and butter pudding wherever there was a group gathering in the name of bereavement.

Pudding

8 slices day-old bread

¼ cup (½ stick) unsalted butter, softened

3 eggs

2 cups warm milk

½ cup granulated sugar

1 teaspoon vanilla extract

½ cup raisins

2 tablespoons ground cinnamon

2 tablespoons sugar

Vanilla Sauce

½ cup granulated sugar

1 tablespoon cornstarch

1 cup water

2 tablespoon unsalted butter

2 teaspoons vanilla extract

Pinch of salt

Preheat the oven to 350°F.

Grease a deep 2-quart baking dish. Set it aside.

To make the pudding, remove the crusts from the bread slices. Lavishly butter the bread slices on one side. Cut the bread slices in half to make 2 triangles, then arrange the triangles, buttered side up, in the prepared dish. In a large bowl, whisk the eggs until they are well mixed. Add the milk, sugar, and vanilla extract to the eggs. Whisk the ingredients well. Stir in the raisins. Slowly pour the custard over the bread, making sure all of the bread is well soaked. Bake for 45 minutes, or until the custard has set. Remove the pudding from the oven. Sprinkle with the cinnamon and sugar.

To make the sauce, combine the sugar and cornstarch in a small bowl. Set the bowl aside. In a small saucepan, bring the water to boil over high heat. Add the sugar and cornstarch mixture to the boiling water; decrease the heat to medium. Stir constantly until the mixture is completely blended. Cook the sauce until it thickens, 3 to 5 minutes, then remove the saucepan from the heat. Add the butter, vanilla extract, and salt. Stir until the butter is melted, then spoon the sauce over the warm or room-temperature pudding and serve.

Serves 6 to 8

Left to right: Miss Essie Brazil, Sister Rose Johnston, Miss Fannie Mae Watts, early 1960s.

OLD-TIME RICE PUDDIN'

This is a traditional southern pudding your family will enjoy. I like it because it's baked in the oven, not cooked on top of the stove. When there are leftovers, I sometimes have a bowl for breakfast.

¾ cup long-grain rice

6 cups milk

1 cup heavy cream

¾ cup granulated sugar

4 egg yolks, beaten

1 teaspoon cornstarch

2 teaspoons vanilla extract

1 teaspoon grated lemon zest (optional)

Ground nutmeg, for sprinkling

Ground cinnamon, for sprinkling

Whipped cream (optional)

Preheat the oven to 350°F.

Lightly grease a 2-quart casserole dish. Set it aside.

In a saucepan, combine the rice and milk. Cook over medium heat until the rice is tender, about 15 minutes. Stir occasionally, making sure the rice does not stick to the bottom of the saucepan. When the rice is tender, decrease the heat. In a bowl, combine the cream, sugar, egg yolks, cornstarch, vanilla extract, and lemon zest. Mix well after each addition. Gradually stir the cream mixture into the rice. Bring the mixture to a boil. Remove the saucepan from the heat and pour the contents into the prepared casserole dish. Sprinkle with nutmeg and cinnamon to suit your taste. Place the casserole in a larger pan filled with enough warm water to come halfway up the sides of the casserole. Bake for 45 minutes, or until the custard is almost set, stirring after 10 minutes, and again after 15 minutes. Remove the casserole from the larger pan and transfer to a wire rack to cool slightly or completely. Serve warm or cold, with whipped cream, if desired.

Serves 6 to 8

BISCUIT PUDDIN'

I'm told that years ago folks made pudding out of their leftover breakfast biscuits. They didn't have much, so they learned to be creative with what they had.

In our family, Pop was the biscuit maker. And I'm here to tell you, the man could have built an empire on the goodness of his biscuits, they were that wonderful. Some Saturday mornings he'd spread the word around that he had a tin of biscuits in the oven and he was about to pop the lid on a jar of My My's homemade fruit preserves. Shortly thereafter, a dozen people were sitting around his table. Later that night, while she was cooking her Sunday-dinner sweets, My My would make biscuit pudding out of the leftovers—if there were any leftovers.

This is an old country recipe; it's delicious and it's comforting.

---

14 biscuits, crumbled

1 cup milk

1 cup half-and-half

¾ cup (1½ sticks) unsalted butter, melted

4 eggs, beaten

1½ cups granulated sugar

½ teaspoon ground cinnamon

½ teaspoon ground nutmeg

1 tablespoon vanilla extract

1 cup raisins

Whipped cream (optional)

Preheat the oven to 350°F.

Grease a 2-quart casserole dish. Set it aside.

Combine the crumbled biscuits, milk, half-and-half, and butter in a large bowl. Soak the biscuits until they are soft, about 3 minutes. Next, add the eggs, sugar, cinnamon, nutmeg, vanilla extract, and raisins; mix well after each addition. Let the mixture stand for 30 minutes, then pour into the prepared baking dish. Bake for 35 to 45 minutes, or until the top of the pudding is golden brown. Remove the pudding from the oven. Serve it hot or cold, with whipped cream, if desired.

Serves 4 to 6

OLD-FASHIONED SWEET POTATO PONE

Just the mention of sweet potato pone conjures up images of my grandmother, my mother, and my aunts the night before an event for which they were preparing dishes. On those nights, the phone lines remained busy as the women measured each other's progress. It was a busy time; husbands and kids with driver's licenses ran to the store for this or for that and dropped off loaf pans and baking tins to those whose concoctions exceeded the boundaries of the bakeware they owned. On those nights, someone in the family was surely making a sweet potato pone. Basically, the filling for sweet potato pone is similar to the filling for sweet potato pie, only it's firmer and it's sliceable. I like to serve my slices topped with whipped cream. Not only does it enhance its flavor, but it also enhances its appearance.

2½ cups milk

4 sweet potatoes, peeled and coarsely grated

3 eggs

2½ cups granulated sugar

½ teaspoon ground cinnamon

¼ teaspoon ground cloves

¼ teaspoon ground nutmeg

1 teaspoon grated orange zest

½ cup chopped pecans

¼ cup (½ stick) unsalted butter, softened

Preheat the oven to 350°F.

Grease a 2-quart casserole dish.

Pour the milk into the prepared casserole dish. Stir the grated sweet potatoes into the milk; this will prevent the potatoes from turning dark. In a mixing bowl, beat the eggs well. Gradually add the sugar, cinnamon, and cloves, mixing well after each addition. Add the nutmeg, orange zest, and pecans. Mix until all of the ingredients are evenly distributed. Pour the mixture into the potato mixture and mix well. Dot the top with butter. Bake for 1 hour and 45 minutes, or until the pudding is set. Remove the dish from the oven. Let the pudding stand for 30 minutes before serving.

Serves 6 to 8

Everything Should Look Its Best

There are certain womanly adages that are particular to a family. *Don't tell a man too much too soon* and *Don't let yourself go; keep yourself up* are the two mottoes from my family that stick out in my mind, especially the latter. Seems like everywhere I went, somebody was reminding me to keep myself up. "If you don't oil your skin it'll dry out." "If you keep bitin' on your nails your hands'll look deformed." "If you don't sit up straight your back'll start to curve." When I was a little girl my grandmother's vanity table was never without what I considered an amazing number of beauty potions for a woman her age—a bottle of Jergens Lotion, a jar of Indian Sage hair pomade, a container of Vaseline, a box of Calgon bubble bath. I'd watch My My cook and clean all day, then, after she'd finished her chores and Pop was sitting at the table with his Bible and his magnifying glass, I'd watch her trudge into the bathroom, hear her light the pilot on the heat stove, and then hear the rush of water. It always amazed me how she dragged herself into the bathroom smelling like collard greens and sweet potato pie, but emerged tipping like a spring chicken and smelling like a bowl of fresh flowers that had just been set out—so much so that even Pop would have to look up from the Good Book and mark her progress as she passed through the room. I used to sit on the bed beside my grandmother as she rubbed herself down with her fragrant ointments. It baffled me because, to me, why bother? She was old. From time to time she would glance down at me, our eyes would meet, and she would say, "Sug, never let yourself go; *always* keep yourself up."

Customarily, soul food desserts are not served with a lot of embellishment. *Delicious* and *unassuming* are words that convey their basic nature. But my family tended to use a lot of garnish—whipped cream, hot or cold sauces, fruit wedges, or ice cream—because they believed that *everything* should look its best.

Cud'n Ethel's
PEACH BREAD PUDDIN'

Cud'n Ethel—My My's cousin three or four times removed—says this is her pastor's favorite dessert when he comes for supper. Says if it weren't for the fact that she hides a good-sized helping for her and her husband, Cud'n Will, way to the back of the oven, the pastor would eat the whole damn thing by himself. Well, truth be told, this isn't exactly how Cud'n Ethel tells it. In all of my days, I've never heard a coarse word stumble out of Cud'n Ethel's mouth. This is how Cud'n Will tells it, when he's telling the story.

This dessert tastes especially good served warm with a good-sized dollop of vanilla ice cream.

½ cup raisins

¼ cup rum

5 eggs, beaten

½ cup granulated sugar

4 cups evaporated milk

¼ cup (½ stick) unsalted butter, melted

1 tablespoon vanilla extract

1 tablespoon ground nutmeg

8 to 10 slices home-style bread, coarsely torn

2½ cups sliced peaches in heavy syrup, drained, plus ⅓ cup of the reserved syrup

Preheat the oven to 350°F.

Lightly grease a 2-quart baking dish. Set it aside.

Place the raisins in a bowl. Set them aside. In a small saucepan, heat the rum over low heat. Pour the heated rum over the raisins and set aside. In a large bowl, combine the eggs, sugar, and milk. Mix until the sugar is dissolved, then add the butter, vanilla extract, and nutmeg. Place the bread in another large bowl. Pour the milk mixture over the bread. Spoon in the peaches. Stir the reserved peach syrup into the raisin mixture. Mix well, then pour the raisin mixture on top of the bread pieces. Gently mix until the ingredients are well combined. Pour the mixture into the prepared baking dish. Bake for 50 minutes, or until the pudding is fluffy and nicely browned. Remove from the oven. Serve warm or at room temperature.

Serves 6 to 8

Aint Marjell's
EGG PUDDIN'

Of my mother's sisters, Aint Marjell was the most worldly. Before she became a licensed beautician, she worked in a popular little Jewish-owned restaurant in our community. In fact, the restaurant, Cooks, was down the street from My My's house; we could sit on My My's porch and watch Aint Marjell through the restaurant's large plate-glass window with her pad and her pencil, waiting on customers and wiping down the boomerang-shaped counter. The restaurant was a favorite of the underworld crowd, both black and white. And it was a favorite of our town's "colored" elite. High-rolling big-time hustlers, number runners, gangsters, and pimps and their girls dined alongside the well-respected preachers, teachers, morticians, and bankers from our community. After work, Aint Marjell would rush home and give us the scoop on what she'd seen and heard that day. More so than the other kids, it seemed, I could hardly wait for her shift to end, for her to walk the block or so down to My My's house to fill us in on that day's happenings at the restaurant. Even back then, I relished hearing snippets about other people's lives—I wasn't nosy, just fascinated. My My swore it was because I had the sense of someone who'd lived before; said she realized it the day I was born. When she peeped inside my blanket and looked deep into my eyes, my eyes were looking back just as deep into hers. She said it startled her so bad it liked to give her a heart attack. Of course, had the grown folks—Big Mama, more than anyone else—really known how fascinated I was with the stories about the people who frequented Cooks restaurant and that I wasn't as engrossed in play as I'd pretend during Aint Marjell's daily accountings, they would have sent me out of the room with the admonishment, "It ain't good for a little girl to hear too much too soon."

Aint Marjell's egg pudding is baked in the oven; most egg puddings that I've seen are cooked on top of the stove.

---

4 eggs, beaten well

1 cup granulated sugar

4 tablespoons all-purpose flour

2 cups milk

3 tablespoons unsalted butter, melted

1 teaspoon vanilla extract

½ teaspoon ground nutmeg

Preheat the oven to 350°F.

Lightly grease an 9-inch pie pan. Set it aside.

In a bowl, beat the eggs and sugar until light and fluffy. Add the flour, milk, butter, and vanilla extract. Mix well. Pour the mixture into the prepared pie pan. Sprinkle the top with nutmeg. Bake for 1 hour, or until a toothpick inserted in the middle comes out clean. Transfer the pudding from the oven to a wire rack. Cool completely before serving.

Note: Once, when My My was running low on sugar, she used a cup of light corn syrup instead. According to My My, nobody knew the difference, "and if they did, it didn't hinder 'em from asking for seconds."

Serves 4 to 6

STOVE-TOP BREAD PUDDIN'

When you have a craving for something simple yet delicious, this stove-top pudding is the perfect dessert. The spices in the raisin-cinnamon bread will save you a bit of preparation time.

2 eggs

1¾ cups milk

1 cup granulated sugar

12 slices raisin-cinnamon bread, coarsely torn, lightly toasted

In a large bowl, combine the eggs, milk, and sugar. Blend well. Pour the mixture into a large nonstick skillet. Add the bread and stir to coat. Continue to stir the bread over low to medium heat, until the pudding is thick. Remove the skillet from the heat. Serve the pudding warm, or at room temperature.

Serves 4

Pop on his side porch with Aint Betty Jean's son, Randy. In the distance is Cooks restaurant. We could sit on the porch and see Aint Marjell at work.

  Sweets

Aint Sarah's
SWEET POTATO DESSERT

Aint Sarah, My My's younger sister who lived in New Orleans, was one of those people who believed in having lots of life insurance coverage. No sooner than a baby was born into the family, she'd rush downtown to the insurance company to take out a policy on her. It used to tickle folks when they learned that not only did she probably have her entire family covered, it was just as likely that she had a policy on the mailman, the milkman, her butcher, her doctor, her dentist, her pastor, her beautician, her neighbors, and the broom salesman, whom she hardly knew. They say Aint Sarah was an extraordinary cook and folks loved it when she called them to supper. They also say she had a good little second income—and that she lived quite well—collecting on her life-insurance policies.

Sweet, rich, and crunchy, Aint Sarah's lovely dessert will grace your table, no matter if you're serving it on a weekday or on a holiday.

Dessert

6 sweet potatoes, cooked, peeled, and mashed

½ cup (1 stick) unsalted butter, melted

1 cup granulated sugar

2 teaspoons vanilla extract

2 eggs

½ cup evaporated milk

½ teaspoon ground cinnamon

½ teaspoon ground nutmeg

½ teaspoon ground ginger

Whipped cream (optional)

Pecan Topping

1½ cups pecans, coarsely chopped

⅓ cup unsalted butter, melted

½ cup all-purpose flour

1 cup firmly packed brown sugar

Preheat the oven to 350°F.

Lightly grease a 9 by 13-inch casserole dish. Set it aside.

To make the dessert, combine the sweet potatoes, butter, sugar, and vanilla extract in a large bowl. Mix well. Add the eggs one at a time, beating well after each addition. Gradually stir in the evaporated milk. Add the cinnamon, nutmeg, and ginger. Mix thoroughly. Spread the sweet potato mixture in the prepared casserole dish.

To make the topping, in a mixing bowl, combine the pecans, butter, flour, and brown sugar. Mix the ingredients with a pastry blender or with your fingers until the mixture forms pea-sized crumbs. Crumble the topping over the dessert. Bake for approximately 45 minutes, or until a toothpick inserted near the center comes out clean. Remove from the oven and let cool on a wire rack.

Serves 4 to 6

Use What You Have

Mama used to say that anything could be made to look stylish if you gave it a little attention. To prove her point, she was always updating her wardrobe, adding lace or rickrack to plain hems, replacing old buttons with new ones, or re-creating the details at the necks and the sleeves of her outfits. She could take a plain old dress that she'd had for years and turn it into something new.

When it came to embellishing the simple puddings and desserts that became my family's culinary trademark, Mama said that nobody could outdo Aint Marjell. She said Aint Marjell could take a paper bag and make it look good enough to eat. Nobody thought to do such creative things with such simple ingredients as Aint Marjell. For instance, Aint Marjell made her plain coffee cakes special by spreading preserves on top of them, then broiling them until they bubbled. When you think about it, I guess that's what we've all been called here to do: to take the little that we're given in life and turn it into something tasteful.

BREAD PUDDIN' UPSIDE DOWN

This simple, tasty dish will comfort your soul.

8 slices day-old white bread, cubed

⅓ cup plus ½ cup granulated sugar

2 cups milk

2 eggs, beaten well

1 teaspoon vanilla extract

1 tablespoon unsalted butter, melted

½ cup pineapple chunks, drained

½ cup slivered almonds

Preheat the oven to 350°F.

Thoroughly grease a 2-quart baking dish. Set it aside.

Place the bread cubes in a large mixing bowl. Set the bowl aside. In a small skillet over low heat, melt the ⅓ cup of sugar until it forms a caramel-like syrup. Stir constantly to avoid scorching. Quickly pour the caramelized sugar into the prepared baking dish, tipping the dish to coat the sides. Then, in a mixing bowl, combine the milk, eggs, the ½ cup sugar, the vanilla extract, and the melted butter. Beat the ingredients until they are well mixed. Stir in the pineapple chunks. Pour the milk mixture over the bread cubes. Spoon the cubes into the baking dish that has been coated with caramelized sugar. Sprinkle the top with almonds. Bake for 35 to 40 minutes, or until a toothpick inserted in the middle comes out clean. Remove from the oven. Immediately unmold the pudding to a serving platter. Serve it warm or cooled.

Serves 4 to 6

Cud'n Bertise (front center) directed a rural Mississippi church choir in the 1950s.

Cud'n Florence's
CORNMEAL PUDDIN'

Every family has a wild woman: a woman who talks loud and saucy and throws her head way back when she laughs; a woman who smooths the seat of her dress in a seductive manner when she walks, seemingly unaware of the folks straining to catch a glimpse; one who may be well past her prime but is obviously still having sex with her husband, and obviously still enjoying it. Cud'n John's wife, Florence, was our family's wild woman. A cross between Eartha Kitt and Moms Mabley, Cud'n Florence was a purring kitten one minute and a court jester the next. She could mimic mannerisms and tell jokes with the precision of a professional comedian. She kept us—including Big Mama, who didn't tolerate too much foolishness—laughing.

There were all kinds of rumors about the way Cud'n John, My My's first cousin on her mama's side, and a dapper, street-smart man in his own right, met Cud'n Florence—there was some real speculation where Cud'n Florence's past was concerned. But all the women in my family loved her anyway. They praised her for the way she kept herself up, and marveled over how neat and clean she kept her house, right down to her chest of drawers, where every bra and every panty was neatly folded the way they are on the display tables in boutiques. And they admired her for the glorious and eclectic way she lived her life— shopping trips to Chicago with the girls, civic club meetings, Friday night card games, and hosting Sunday afternoon church socials.

Cud'n Florence might have been our family's wild woman, but now that I am older and things make more sense, I understand that she was way more than just our family's wild woman. Cud'n Florence was also a model, of sorts, for the women in my family. When Cud'n Florence came to town—she and Cud'n John lived in a lovely old home in Detroit—all the women, including Big Mama, gathered around her. Her loud laughter, her sauciness, her accounts of her latest adventures and investments, and the sexy way she put her hand on her hip when she took a glass of ice water to Cud'n John mesmerized us. In Cud'n Florence, young and old, we saw our feminine possibilities. In her we witnessed an older woman who still flaunted her feminine curves, one who was full of joy, full of seasoned feminine grace, aware of it, proud of it, and overflowing with love.

Cud'n Florence brought this delicious pudding to all of our family dinners. She would bring the pudding to the table, warmed, along with a pitcher of heavy cream that she'd sweetened to suit her taste, then we'd pour what we wanted over our portion. Sometimes, I'd ask to have a scoop of vanilla ice cream put on top of mine.

1 cup yellow cornmeal

4½ cups milk

1 cup firmly packed brown sugar

½ cup dark molasses

¼ cup (½ stick) unsalted butter

¼ teaspoon salt

¼ teaspoon baking soda

2 eggs, beaten

1 teaspoon ground ginger

½ teaspoon ground nutmeg

½ teaspoon ground cinnamon

Preheat the oven to 300°F.

Grease a 2-quart casserole dish. Set it aside.

Pour the cornmeal into a large saucepan. Add 1½ cups of the milk and stir thoroughly. Add the sugar, molasses, butter, salt, baking soda, and eggs, mixing well after each addition. Add the ginger, nutmeg, and cinnamon to the cornmeal mixture. Blend well, then set the pan aside. In another large saucepan, scald the remaining 3 cups milk over low heat, cooking until it is hot but not yet boiling. Gradually stir the hot milk into the cornmeal mixture and cook over low heat for about 10 minutes, or until the mixture is the consistency of hot cereal. Stir constantly to prevent lumps. Pour the cornmeal mixture into the prepared casserole dish. Bake for 2½ hours. Remove from the oven and let the pudding stand for 3 to 4 hours before serving.

Serves 6 to 8

Left, Uncle Joe; *right,* Pop.

My dad's mother, Mary Lee Stubblefield, and my dad's stepfather, Grandaddy George, with their foster children, early 1960s.

Cookies & Candies

Left to right: Big Mama, her cooking rival Sister Hewlett, my mother, Aint Helen, 1960s.

When I was a little girl, My My once said, "A woman is a powerful thang, but most women don't know it." When she said it, it was Saturday night; she was sitting at the kitchen table, watching over her Sunday sweets as they cooked in the oven, and talking long-distance to Cud'n Mayetta, one of My My's younger Mississippi cousins. I don't believe the other children who were in the room were paying attention to My My's conversation; they were too busy stirring, and chopping, and grating (on Saturday nights, My My was the head chef and my cousins and I were her little sous-chefs, working according to her instructions), but I took notice. For some reason, even though I was just a little girl, I knew the message was meant as much for me as it was for Cud'n Mayetta. "'Cause if women knew just *how* powerful they were," My My continued, "they wouldn't be so quick to fall to pieces every time a man shows his ass."

In My My's house, there was always a china dish of homemade cookies or a glass candy bowl of handspun confection sitting on a coffee table or resting on the wide arm of an easy chair. It was different back then. Women had different attitudes about femininity and about its sweeping power. Women *knew* what they were doing when they set a pretty table, arranged a bowl of fresh flowers on the dinner table, or placed a warm rug near the water faucet. They were attuned to the feminine power in the so-called little things that they did to make their homes warm and loving.

When I was a little girl, I learned a lot about womanly power in My My's kitchen. The women in my family often gathered there to do their woman talk. My My preached her womanly sermons to her girls at her kitchen-table pulpit. They were always sermons of domestic power, not ones of kitchen drudgery. My My used to say, "A plate of homemade tea cakes or a bowl of fresh-made bean fudge can work wonders on an ailing marriage."

Looking back, I remember how quickly the mood changed when my grandmother carried a plate of her delectable homemade confections into a room where the boys and the men were gathered. They were in awe of her ability to read moods: *How could she know that this is just what we needed at this precise moment?* The pleasantly surprised look that spread over their faces is where I first glimpsed the power of the feminine that My My was always talking about.

Me with my childhood sidekick, my cousin Ernest, early 1960s.

Miss Rosa Lee's
OATMEAL COOKIES

Miss Rosa Lee, a tall, light-skinned woman who wore thick sienna-colored face powder and cat-eye glasses with rhinestone rims, was our family's piano teacher. She came to My My's house on Saturday mornings at the crack of dawn, with a metal pointer and a leather satchel full of classical sheet music. My My would lead her into the family room where the upright player piano stood in one corner, then one by one, we each entered the room for our lessons, even My My and Big Mama.

A native of Chicago, Miss Rosa met and married her husband, Mr. Henry, shortly after she moved to our small town. By the time she came to town, she was well into the prime of her life. Her new husband was considered a good catch for a woman that age; he owned a lovely old home, he received a sizable pension from General Motors, and he wasn't too bad to look at. Everyone wondered what it was about Miss Rosa that had enabled her to capture the heart of a man whom a lot of local women had been trying to capture for years.

Mama used to say, "There ain't nothin' special about Miss Rosa. She was new in town, a woman folks didn't know anything about; that's what attracted Mr. Henry. Nobody could say they had anything on her. Just goes to show you, sometimes a woman has to leave town, go where don't nobody know anything about her, to attract a good man."

Miss Rosa's oatmeal cookies hold a hint of cinnamon. That's what makes them so aromatic; fresh baked, they make your house smell good. For variation, I sometimes add a cup of raisins.

½ cup vegetable oil

½ cup (1 stick) unsalted butter, softened

1 cup firmly packed light brown sugar

1 cup granulated sugar

2 eggs

1 teaspoon vanilla extract

2 teaspoons ground cinnamon

1 teaspoon baking soda

1 teaspoon baking powder

2 cups all-purpose flour

2 cups rolled oats

1 cup walnuts or pecans, chopped

Preheat the oven to 350°F.

In a large bowl, cream together the oil, butter, and brown and white sugars until the mixture is light and fluffy. Add the eggs one at a time, beating well after each addition. Blend in the vanilla extract, cinnamon, baking soda, and baking powder. Add the flour, rolled oats, and nuts. Mix until the ingredients are well blended. Drop the dough by the teaspoonful on ungreased cookie sheets. Bake for 10 to 12 minutes, or until the cookies are golden brown. Remove the cookies from the oven and allow to cool on the cookie sheet for 5 minutes before transferring them to a wire rack to cool completely.

Makes 3 dozen cookies

Cud'n Eunice's
OLD-FASHIONED TEA CAKES

Tea cakes are the ultimate soul food cookie. Cud'n Eunice's tea cakes were everyone's favorite because they were lightly spiced and they weren't too sweet. They go so well with a glass of ice-cold milk.

1 cup (2 sticks) unsalted butter, softened, or 1 cup vegetable shortening

1½ cups granulated sugar

3 eggs

3½ cups all-purpose flour

2 teaspoons baking powder

1 teaspoon ground nutmeg

½ cup buttermilk

½ cup light molasses

1 teaspoon vanilla extract

Preheat the oven to 350°F.

Lightly grease 2 cookie sheets. Set them aside.

In a large mixing bowl, cream together the butter and sugar. Stir in the eggs one at a time, beating well after each addition, then set the bowl aside. In another bowl, sift together the flour, baking powder, and nutmeg. Set the bowl aside. Pour the buttermilk into another bowl. Pour the molasses into the buttermilk. Add the vanilla extract and mix well. Add the flour mixture, a cup at a time, to the butter mixture, alternating with the buttermilk mixture. Mix until a smooth dough forms. Roll the dough out on a generously floured surface and then gather together to form a ball. Roll the dough out again, repeating this process 3 to 4 times. Roll out the dough ½ inch thick, then cut with a drinking glass or a round cookie cutter. Bake the tea cakes on the greased cookie sheets for 8 to 10 minutes, or until slightly brown. Remove the tea cakes from the oven and allow to cool on the cookie sheet for 5 minutes before transferring them to a wire rack to cool completely.

Note: For a variation, I sometimes substitute lemon or almond extract for the vanilla extract.

Makes 2 to 3 dozen cookies

My My's
OLD-FASHIONED GINGERSNAPS

A pinch of black pepper adds to the spiciness of these thin cookies, Pop's favorite. My My always kept a batch on hand.

1 cup granulated sugar, plus more for coating

¾ cup (1½ sticks) unsalted butter or butter-flavored vegetable shortening

1 egg

¼ cup dark molasses

1 teaspoon vanilla extract

2 cups all-purpose flour

2 teaspoons baking soda

1 teaspoon ground ginger

½ teaspoon ground cinnamon

½ teaspoon ground cloves

Pinch of salt

Pinch of ground black pepper

Lightly grease 2 cookie sheets. Set them aside.

In a large bowl, cream together the 1 cup sugar and the butter until the mixture is smooth. Beat in the egg, molasses, and vanilla extract until the ingredients are well blended. In another large bowl, sift together the flour, baking soda, ginger, cinnamon, cloves, salt, and the black pepper. Stir the sifted flour mixture into the molasses mixture to form a dough. Wrap the dough in plastic, then chill for at least 1 hour for easier handling.

Preheat the oven to 350°F. Remove the chilled dough from the refrigerator. Roll the dough into 1-inch balls, then roll the balls in the granulated sugar. Place the balls on the prepared cookie sheets about 2 inches apart and bake for 8 to 10 minutes, or until the cookies are crisp but not dark. Remove the cookies from the oven and allow to cool on the cookie sheet for 5 minutes before transferring them to a wire rack to cool completely.

Makes 3 dozen cookies

My My's father, Rance Dixon. Everyone called him Papa.

Aint Weezy's
PEANUT BUTTER COOKIES

Eloise, My My's baby sister, wasn't much older than her nieces, my mother and my mother's sisters. When they were little girls, Mama and her sisters played London Bridge is falling down, little Sally Walker, and ring-around-the-rosy with their little Aint Weezy. Mama said it was hard for her and her sisters to think of little Weezy as their ainty, since she was just a year older than Mama. Years later, My My would say of her baby sister, "Weezy grow'd up to be a good little cook."

These cookies are delicious and they always turn out.

---

1 cup (2 sticks) unsalted butter, softened

1 cup smooth peanut butter

1 cup firmly packed light brown sugar

1 cup granulated sugar, plus more for sprinkling

2 eggs

2½ cups all-purpose flour

¼ teaspoon salt

½ teaspoon baking powder

Preheat the oven to 350°F.

Lightly grease 2 cookie sheets. Set them aside.

Combine the butter, peanut butter, brown sugar, and the 1 cup granulated sugar in a large mixing bowl. Add the eggs one at a time, beating well after each addition. In another large bowl, sift together the flour, salt, and baking powder. Gradually stir the flour mixture into the peanut butter mixture until the ingredients are well blended. Drop the dough by the spoonful onto the prepared cookie sheet. Flatten each mound with a fork, then sprinkle lightly with granulated sugar. Bake for 12 to 14 minutes, or until the cookies are lightly browned. Remove the cookies from the oven and allow to cool on the cookie sheet for 5 minutes before transferring them to a wire rack to cool completely.

Makes 3 to 4 dozen cookies

Grandmother Stubblefield's
OLD-FASHIONED SUGAR COOKIES

Grandmother Stubblefield was my father's mother. Her Indian ancestry was evidenced in the wavy texture of her jet-black hair and in the striking features of her cream-colored face. She was an excellent cook who raised tons of foster children, several of whom went on to become doctors and lawyers. Grandmother Stubblefield, who cooked her meals in the largest pots and the widest pans that I had ever seen, made the best rolled sugar cookies in the world. Even My My said so. And Lord knows My My wouldn't compliment your cooking if it didn't deserve it.

2 cups granulated sugar, plus more for sprinkling

1 cup vegetable shortening

1 teaspoon baking powder

1 teaspoon cream of tartar

1 teaspoon ground nutmeg

3 eggs

1 cup buttermilk

1 teaspoon baking soda

5½ cups all-purpose flour

1 teaspoon vanilla extract

Grease 2 cookie sheets. Set them aside.

Place the sugar, the shortening, baking powder, cream of tartar, and nutmeg in a large bowl. Blend until the ingredients are well distributed. Add the eggs to the mixture one at a time, beating well after each addition. In a bowl, combine the buttermilk and baking soda. Stir until the baking soda is blended into the buttermilk. Pour the buttermilk mixture into the sugar mixture. Add the flour 1 cup at a time, beating well with an electric mixer on medium speed after each addition. Cover and refrigerate the dough for 1 hour.

Preheat the oven to 350°F. Remove the chilled dough from the refrigerator. Roll the dough out on a well-floured surface to a ¼-inch thickness and cut into rounds with a biscuit cutter. Place the dough rounds 2 inches apart on the prepared cookie sheet and bake for 8 to 10 minutes, or until the cookies are light brown. Remove them from the oven and sprinkle with granulated sugar (or colored sugars during the holidays). Allow the cookies to cool on the cookie sheet for 5 minutes before transferring them to a wire rack to cool completely.

Makes 4 to 5 dozen cookies

Cud'n Daisy's
GOOD OL' CHOCOLATE CHIP COOKIES

Cud'n Daisy was a pretend cousin (in the South, folks would claim a person as kin simply because they liked the person). Even though she wasn't true kin, we couldn't have loved Cud'n Daisy more had she been genuinely related to us. When we rejoiced, she rejoiced; when we mourned, she mourned. They say Cud'n Daisy was as lucky in love as any woman could hope to be. They say she'd had well over five husbands (whoever was telling the story would start counting them off on their fingers). No sooner than one would go to be with the Lord, or to be with another woman, Cud'n Daisy would hitch up with another fine man. My My once asked her for her secret. (I'm sure My My was thinking of poor Cud'n Ophelia, who was unmarried and getting on in age, when she asked.) Cud'n Daisy's reply was, "Smile as often as you can. Laugh frequently. When you talk to a man, look him directly in the eye. Be kind. Don't be afraid to chase after him, but remember: for every two steps that you move forward, you need to take two steps backward. In other words, chase after him awhile, then stop and let him chase you a stretch. And once you get him, if you have a house dog, don't let it outdo you when it comes to showin' the man how glad you are to see him come home. When the doggie hears his car pull up and comes runnin' through the house like a fool, be waiting at the door beside the dog."

Every now and then Cud'n Daisy would pack a big batch of her delicious chocolate chip cookies into a shoe box lined with tinfoil and airmail them to us, all the way from Mississippi. Mama liked Cud'n Daisy's sweet and gooey chocolate chip cookies so much that she asked for the recipe.

1½ cups (3 sticks) unsalted butter, softened

1¼ cups firmly packed brown sugar

1¼ cups granulated sugar

3 eggs

2 teaspoons vanilla extract

4 cups all-purpose flour

2 teaspoons baking soda

⅛ teaspoon salt

2 cups semisweet chocolate chips

2 cups walnuts, chopped

Preheat the oven to 350°F.

In a large bowl, cream together the butter and the brown and the white sugars. Beat the mixture until it's light and fluffy. Add the eggs one at a time, beating well after each addition, then stir in the vanilla extract. Continue to blend until the mixture is smooth. Add the flour, baking soda, and salt to the mixture. Blend well. Stir in the chocolate chips and the walnuts until they are evenly distributed throughout the dough. Drop the dough by tablespoonfuls onto ungreased cookie sheets about 1 inch apart. Bake for 8 to 10 minutes, or until the cookies are golden brown. Remove the cookies from the oven and allow to cool on the cookie sheet for at least 5 minutes before transferring them to a wire rack to cool completely.

Makes 4 dozen cookies

Mama's
SPICE COOKIES

Freshly grated ginger gives these cookies a little zip. Mama used to put these in my lunch box and before I got to school, they were gone. That's how much I liked them.

1¼ cups vegetable shortening

1½ cups granulated sugar, plus more for coating

6 tablespoons molasses

2 eggs

1 teaspoon finely grated fresh ginger

3¼ cups all-purpose flour

1 teaspoon ground cloves

1 teaspoon ground cinnamon

2 teaspoons baking soda

Grease 2 cookie sheets. Set them aside.

In a large bowl, cream together the shortening and the 1½ cups sugar. Add the molasses, eggs, and ginger. Beat well. In another large bowl, sift together the flour, cloves, cinnamon, and baking soda. Gradually stir the dry ingredients into the shortening mixture. Stir until the mixture is smooth. Cover and refrigerate the dough for 1 hour, or until it is firm enough to handle.

Preheat the oven to 375°F. Roll the chilled dough into 1-inch balls; roll each ball in granulated sugar. Place the balls on the prepared cookie sheets. Bake for 10 to 12 minutes, or until the cookies are lightly browned around the edges. Remove the cookies from the oven and allow to cool on the cookie sheet for 5 minutes before transferring them to a wire rack to cool completely.

Makes 4 dozen cookies

Mama, 1960s.

  Sweets

WALNUT COOKIES

I love these cookies! The walnut topping really sets them apart.

Cookies

½ cup (1 stick) unsalted butter, softened

1 (3-ounce) package cream cheese, softened

2 tablespoons sour cream

1 cup granulated sugar

1 egg

1 teaspoon vanilla extract

2 cups all-purpose flour

½ teaspoon baking powder

⅛ teaspoon salt

1 cup walnuts, finely chopped

Walnut Topping

¼ cup firmly packed brown sugar

3 tablespoons unsalted butter, softened

½ cup walnuts, chopped

To make the cookies, in a bowl, beat the butter, cream cheese, and sour cream until the mixture is smooth. Add the sugar and continue beating until well blended. Add the egg and vanilla extract and beat well. Stir in the flour, baking powder, salt, and walnuts. Form the dough into a ball, then flatten it and cover it with plastic wrap. Refrigerate the dough for 3 to 4 hours.

Preheat the oven to 350°F. Remove the chilled dough from the refrigerator. Form the dough into 1-inch balls. Place each ball 2 inches apart on ungreased cookie sheets. With a teaspoon, make a depression in the center of each ball.

To make the walnut topping, in a bowl, blend together the brown sugar and butter. Add the walnuts. Stir until all of the ingredients are well blended. Place a dollop of the topping in each depression in the cookie dough. Bake for 10 to 12 minutes, or until the edges become lightly browned. Remove the cookies from the oven and allow to cool on the cookie sheet for 5 minutes before transferring them to a wire rack to cool completely.

Makes 3 dozen cookies

ORANGE TEA CAKES

Orange tea cakes go well with a glass of ice-cold milk. Make a platter of these moist, almost cakelike cookies, and watch them disappear—even the crumbs.

¾ cup (1½ sticks) unsalted butter, softened

1½ cups granulated sugar

3 eggs

3¾ cups all-purpose flour, plus more for rolling

1 teaspoon baking powder

½ teaspoon salt

1 teaspoon baking soda

1 cup buttermilk

Grated zest of 1 orange

2 tablespoons freshly squeezed orange juice

1 teaspoon vanilla extract

Confectioners' sugar, for dusting

Lightly grease 2 cookie sheets. Set them aside.

In a large bowl, cream the butter and sugar until they are light and well mixed. Add the eggs one at a time, beating well after each addition. In another large bowl, sift together the flour, baking powder, and salt. Set the bowl aside. In another bowl, stir the baking soda into the buttermilk until the baking soda is dissolved. Gradually pour the buttermilk into the butter mixture, alternating with the flour mixture and ending with the buttermilk. Beat the orange zest and the orange juice into the dough. Cover and chill the dough for 1 hour.

Preheat the oven to 350°F. Take the chilled dough out of the refrigerator. Adding more flour is necessary, roll the dough out to a 2-inch thickness and cut into 2-inch rounds. Place the rounds 2 inches apart on the prepared cookie sheet. Bake for 10 to 12 minutes, or until the cookies are light brown around the edges. Remove from the oven and allow the cookies to cool for 5 minutes before transferring them to a wire rack to cool completely. Dust with confectioners' sugar before serving.

Makes 3 dozen cookies

Cud'n Caldin's
BUTTER COOKIES WITH
CINNAMON TOPPING

Cud'n Caldin was the most glamorous woman in our family. It wasn't because she was outwardly beautiful, or because she sang in the 1960s Motown group the Velvelettes, or because she was married to one of the Temptations. We were in awe of Cud'n Caldin because she never let herself loom larger than the rest of us. When she came to family gatherings she could have bragged about the diamond life that she lived, could have gone on and on about the fancy cars, the expensive clothes, and the glittery, high-class folks that she ran around with out in California, but she didn't. She'd sweep into the room in that classy manner that show people have, she'd hug and kiss on us, and then she'd commence helping out in the kitchen, as if she'd never left home. Although she could have spent her time boasting about the things that were going on in her life, when Cud'n Caldin came to town she seemed more interested in what was going on in ours. And that made her all the more glamorous. Big Mama used to say, "Pretty is as pretty does."

These rich little jewels with their cinnamon topping were a family favorite at picnics. The cinnamon topping makes them as pretty as they are delicious.

Cookies

1 cup granulated sugar

1 cup (2 sticks) unsalted butter, softened

2 eggs

2 teaspoons vanilla extract

2 teaspoons almond extract

2½ cups all-purpose flour

1 teaspoon baking powder

Cinnamon-Sugar Topping

4 tablespoons granulated sugar

1 tablespoon ground cinnamon

Lightly grease 2 cookie sheets. Set them aside.

To make the cookies, in a large bowl beat the sugar and butter with an electric mixer until they are light and fluffy. Add the eggs and the vanilla and almond extracts. Beat well. Gradually add the flour and baking powder. Mix the ingredients until a smooth dough forms. Cover and refrigerate the dough for at least 2 hours.

Preheat the oven to 350°F. Remove the chilled dough from the refrigerator. Shape the dough into 1-inch balls.

To make the cinnamon-sugar topping, combine the sugar and cinnamon in a small bowl. Mix with a wire whisk until they are thoroughly blended.

Roll each ball of dough in the topping. Place 2 inches apart on the prepared cookie sheets. Refrigerate for 30 minutes, then bake for 6 to 10 minutes, or until the edges of the cookies are lightly browned. Remove the cookies from the oven and allow them to cool on the cookie sheet for 5 minutes before transferring them to a wire rack to cool completely.

Makes 3 dozen cookies

Sister Hewlett's
MOLASSES SUGAR COOKIES

Sister Hewlett lived a few houses away from Big Mama. In an era where women held each other's domestic prowess to the light, Sister Hewlett and Big Mama were true domestic rivals. Although they called themselves friends, more than anything, they were cooking rivals; they put you in mind of Aunt Bee and her girlfriend, Clara, from the Andy Griffith Show.

In the summer, Sister Hewlett, a plump light-skinned woman who wore the prettiest flower-patterned aprons you ever wanted to see, would mosey on over to where Big Mama was either hanging wash or weeding the vegetable garden in her backyard. They would make a few attempts at chitchat and then the true nature of Sister Hewlett's visit—domestic competition between two countrywomen—would unfold. Big Mama would say, "Sister Hewlett, what 'cha cook good, today?" In a staged nonchalant voice, Sister Hewlett would answer, "Oh, I just threw a little something together . . . smothered chicken and dumplings, a pot of ham hocks and collard greens, a skillet of fried corn, a pan of cornbread, and a batch of molasses cookies, nothing much. What about you? What'd you cook good today, Sister Evans?"

Big Mama would feign a little sigh, her way of letting Sister Hewlett know that she wasn't impressed, and then would say, "I know just what you mean. This was one of them days that I didn't do much more than hit a lick at a stick, my own self. I smoked a pork roast, smothered a cabbage, made a pan of macaroni and cheese, fixed a pot of pinto beans, baked a pound cake, fried some hot-water bread, and made a kettle of sun tea. That's all I had time for after I finished puttin' up twenty-five jars of sweet peas."

This is a delectable, spicy sugar cookie that captures the essence of a down-home dessert. Unbeknown to Big Mama, Aint Marjell, who sampled Sister Hewlett's sugar cookies at a church bake sale, asked her for the recipe.

---

1 cup vegetable shortening or
   unsalted butter, softened

1 cup plus ¼ cup granulated
   sugar

1 egg

¼ cup molasses

2 cups all-purpose flour

2 teaspoons baking soda

1 teaspoon ground cinnamon

½ teaspoon ground cloves

½ teaspoon ground ginger

⅛ teaspoon ground allspice

½ teaspoon salt

Preheat the oven to 350°F.

Lightly grease 2 cookie sheets. Set them aside.

In a large bowl, cream together the shortening, the 1 cup of sugar, egg, and molasses. In another bowl, sift together the flour, baking soda, cinnamon, cloves, ginger, allspice, and salt. Gradually add the flour mixture to the shortening mixture, blending thoroughly after each addition. Lightly flour your hands and roll the dough into 1-inch balls. Roll the balls in the ¼ cup sugar. Place the balls 2 inches apart on the prepared cookie sheets. Make a thumb imprint in each ball and sprinkle a bit more sugar in each thumb print. Bake 8 to 10 minutes for chewy cookies, 10 to 12 minutes for crisper cookies. Remove the cookies from the oven and allow to cool on the cookie sheets for at least 5 minutes before transferring them to a wire rack to cool completely.

Note: When I want to turn out very chewy cookies, I bake them the minimum amount of time called for, then let them cool directly on a platter instead of a wire rack.

Makes 4 dozen cookies

Aint Plute's
BOILED COOKIES

No one knows how My My's aunt, Laura, acquired the nickname "Plute." They say she was a hard little knot of a woman who had been widowed early on. Not only was Aint Plute an excellent cook, but she was also an excellent farmer. They say she and her mule, Pete, could plow a patch of land as good as any man could.

2 cups granulated sugar

½ cup milk

½ cup (1 stick) butter

½ cup cocoa powder

3 cups quick-cooking oats

1 cup chopped nuts

1 teaspoon vanilla extract

Combine the sugar, milk, butter, and cocoa in a large saucepan. Bring to a boil over medium heat. Boil for 2 minutes, then remove the pan from the heat. Add the oats, nuts, and vanilla extract. Stir well. Drop the cookies by the teaspoonful onto waxed paper. Let them stand until they are firm, about 10 minutes.

Makes about 4 dozen cookies

Mama's
CAKE MIX COOKIES

When Mama had a tooth for something sweet, quick, and easy she would often make cake mix cookies.

1 (18.5-ounce) box cake mix,
   any flavor

1 cup vegetable oil

2 eggs

½ teaspoon vanilla extract

Preheat the oven to 350°F.

Lightly grease 2 cookie sheets. Set them aside.

In a large bowl, combine the cake mix, oil, eggs, and vanilla extract. Beat until the ingredients are well blended. Drop the dough by rounded teaspoonfuls onto the prepared baking sheets. Bake for 8 to 10 minutes, or until the cookies are lightly browned around the edges. Remove the cookies from the oven and transfer to wire racks to cool.

> *Note:* For variety, Mama would often add 1 or 2 of the following items to the batter: 1 cup chopped nuts, 1 cup mini semisweet chocolate chips, 1 cup butterscotch chips, 1 cup toffee chips, 1 cup peanut butter chips, ½ cup raisins, ½ cup of sweetened flaked coconut.

Makes 2½ to 3 dozen cookies

My mother's cousin Lillie Bea (background) passing through the neighborhood. Lillie Bea wore dress-up clothes every day of the week.

Big Mama's
BLACK WALNUT BRITTLE

During the Christmas season we looked forward to getting our annual telephone call from Big Mama. "You can stop by and pick up your gift," she'd say in that no-nonsense tone of hers. "It's wrapped and a'waitin'." Why she bothered wrapping her gifts to the family so meticulously was a wonder. Every year we knew exactly what we were getting, because each year Big Mama gave us the same thing—a tin of her delicious, buttery, black walnut brittle.

1 cup granulated sugar

½ cup light corn syrup

¼ cup water

Pinch of salt

½ cup (1 stick) unsalted butter

1½ cups chopped black walnuts

½ teaspoon rum extract

Grease a 10 by 15-inch baking pan. Set it aside.

In a large, heavy saucepan, cook the sugar, corn syrup, and water over medium heat until the sugar dissolves and the mixture comes to a boil. Turn the heat off and let the mixture stand until the bubbles leave. Return to medium heat, add the salt, and beat until thick. Add the butter and cook, stirring occasionally, until the mixture reaches 280°F on a candy thermometer. Stir in the walnuts and rum extract and beat until fairly stiff. Cook until the mixture reaches 300°F. Immediately pour the brittle into the prepared pan. When it's cool, break into pieces.

Makes 1½ pounds candy

Cud'n Sue's
PUDDIN' FUDGE

Cud'n Sue was the sweetest and most gentle person you'd ever want to meet. When she came to visit, her peaceful and loving essence remained in our homes long after she left. However—there's no sweet or delicate way to put it—Cud'n Sue was an afternoon sipper. Corn liquor was her drink of choice. They say if Cud'n Sue heard tell the sheriff was in the neighborhood, she'd quickly hide her liquor barrels in the woods out back, then run up front to her rocking chair, just in time to offer the sheriff a sweet country wave and a polite, "Howdy, Sheriff. Sho' is good to know we got decent folk like you watchin' over us," as he cruised by.

Whenever Cud'n Sue came North for a visit, we'd ask her to make a batch of her delicious fudge. The dark brown sugar that her recipe calls for gives this fudge a sweet, robust flavor.

---

1 small (3.5-ounce) package chocolate pudding mix (heat and serve, not the instant kind)

½ cup evaporated milk

1 cup granulated sugar

½ cup light corn syrup

1 tablespoon unsalted butter

2 tablespoons cornstarch

½ cup chopped walnuts

1½ cups confectioners' sugar

Grease a 9-inch square pan. Set it aside.

In a large saucepan, dissolve the pudding in the milk over low heat, stirring constantly. Add the sugar, corn syrup, and butter. Bring the mixture to a boil, and cook for 5 to 7 minutes, until the mixture reaches 238° on a candy thermometer. Remove the pan from the heat, stir in the cornstarch and the chopped nuts. Gradually stir in the confectioners' sugar. Pour into the prepared pan and let cool until firm. Cut into squares for serving.

Makes about 1 pound fudge

My My's cousin Sue, early 1960s.

CASHEW BRITTLE

When I was a little girl, there were two magazines that I fell in love with. One was Better Homes & Gardens *and the other was* True Confessions. *Aint Helen had given My My a subscription to* Better Homes & Gardens *and Mama's older friend, Miss Ruthie, had given Mama a box full of old* True Confessions. *My My proudly displayed her* Better Homes *on the marble-topped coffee table in her family room. Mama kept her* True Confessions *put away somewhere.*

I enjoyed looking through My My's magazines; sometimes I would draw her attention to a picture in the magazine and she would immediately start the oven and send me to the market to fetch the ingredients the recipe called for. I liked looking at the happy housewives showing off their beautiful homes and their well-trimmed gardens in My My's magazines. Truth be told, when I discovered Mama's magazines pushed to the back of a seldom-used closet, I liked looking at them just as much. (I had to sneak the magazines out of their hiding place one at a time, though, and then carefully place them back the way I'd found them. Mama thought the subject matter was a little too grown for me.) As a little girl, I was fascinated by the women who were bold enough to write: "I Fell in Love with the Man Next Door," "I Kissed the Mailman," and "Sometimes I Feel Like Leaving My Husband and Moving Far Away." What kind of woman would write such a bold thing?

When I was a little girl, I thought the disparities between the happy-faced women in My My's magazine and the weary-looking women who confessed their secrets in Mama's True Confessions *were so wide, they distinguished the women from each another. I had no idea that the smiley-faced women in My My's magazine could very well have been the ones confessing their secrets in Mama's. I was just a little girl; I didn't know.*

This brittle is adapted from a recipe in one of Mama's True Confessions *magazines. The recipe requires that you move quickly. Make sure you have all of the ingredients measured and ready because once you get started, you don't have time to mess around.*

---

1 cup light corn syrup

2¼ cups granulated sugar

1 cup (2 sticks) unsalted butter

1 cup water

3 cups unsalted, raw, coarsely chopped cashews

1½ teaspoons baking soda, sifted

1 teaspoon vanilla extract

Generously grease 2 large baking sheets; set them aside.

In a heavy saucepan, combine the corn syrup, sugar, butter, and water. Stir the ingredients to blend. Cook over medium-high heat, bringing the mixture to a boil. Continue cooking, stirring constantly, for about 10 minutes, or until the mixture registers 250°F on a candy thermometer. Stir in the cashews, increase the heat to high, and continue cooking, stirring frequently, until the mixture registers 300°F. Remove the pan from the heat. Quickly sprinkle in the baking soda, stirring constantly.

(continued)

(continued from page 129)

Add the vanilla extract and stir to distribute the vanilla extract and the baking soda throughout the mixture. Working quickly, pour the mixture onto the baking sheets and spread as evenly as possible. Cool completely on a wire rack, then break the brittle into pieces before serving.

Makes about 1½ pounds candy

A Man in the House

Big Mama once passed through the room where my little cousins and I were setting up our baby dolls and our toy dishes in order to play house. Just as she passed through the room she heard me volunteer to run next door to fetch Billy. Since he was the only boy in the neighborhood who liked playing house as much as we did, he made a wonderful husband.

Big Mama said, "If I was y'all I wouldn't be stuttin' no husband. I'd let Billy stay right where he is. Having a husband is more than a notion. You gotta cook his meals, set his place at the table, wash and iron his clothes, keep after him to stay on top of his health, look over his shoulder to make sure folks ain't takin' advantage of his hospitality. And if that ain't enough, you gotta constantly remind him to leave his street shoes at the door."

When Big Mama made it to the adjacent room, and we could hear the whining of Windex and balled-up newspaper against the picture window and the moaning and groaning of one of her homemade hymns, we talked it over. Eventually, we decided that we could do without a husband or a daddy for our baby dolls that day.

But the next time we played house at Big Mama's, I sneaked next door and got Billy. Regardless of what Big Mama said, playing house was just more fun when there was a husband and a daddy around, someone to delight in the special little things—the tea cakes and the fudge made of mud—that we'd done to make our little playhouse feel more like a home.

Cud'n Bertise's
MASHED POTATO FUDGE

They say that when it came to making love charms and reciting amorous incantations, My My's first cousin, Cud'n Bertise, was one of the best. Folks (black and white, rich and poor) who'd heard tell of her root-work magic came from several counties over, with the assurance that if anybody could mix them up a potion to lure their wandering mates back home, it was Cud'n Bertise. They say weeping wives and disgruntled husbands came at all times of day and night seeking her magic words and formulas. They say Cud'n Bertise would go to the woods in back of her house and commence picking herbs and pulling up roots, and in no time she would whip up something that was powerful enough to travel clear up North— if it had to—to fetch a wayward lover and bring him or her back home. They say folks sure were disappointed when all of a sudden Cud'n Bertise got stirred by the Holy Spirit and declared that what she had been doing all those years was the devil's work. They say she told every one of her customers, "I done all the work for the devil that I'm go'nst to do. From now on, I'm workin' for the Lord."

They say out of all the folks who were disappointed that Bertise would no longer help them, there wasn't none more disappointed than Cud'n Persephine, who had, up until that point, declared Cud'n Bertise's magic nothing more than a bunch of hocus-pocus. Right about the time that Cud'n Bertise went out of the love potion business, rumor had it that Cud'n Persephine's husband, Cud'n Buddy, started keeping some rather late hours. They tell me Cud'n Persephine had a sudden change of heart about Cud'n Bertise's hocus-pocus, and she was willing to try anything—candles, roots, magic words, whatever it took—to keep Cud'n Buddy from getting too attached to whatever it was that was luring him away from home.

Cud'n Bertise started cooking late in life because for so long she was busy tending to the romantic needs of others. Her recipe for mashed potato fudge is richly flavored.

---

3 ounces unsweetened chocolate

¼ cup (½ stick) unsalted butter

½ cup unseasoned mashed potatoes

1 teaspoon vanilla extract

Pinch of salt

1 (1-pound) box confectioners' sugar

1 to 2 teaspoons milk

1 cup chopped walnuts

Grease an 8-inch square pan. Set it aside.

In a large saucepan, melt the chocolate and butter over low heat. Remove the pan from the heat and add the mashed potatoes, vanilla extract, and salt. Mix well. In a large bowl, sift the confectioners' sugar. Add the chocolate mixture to the confectioners' sugar. Mix well; the mixture will be crumbly. Add 1 to 2 teaspoons of milk, if necessary, to make a mixture that can be kneaded. Knead the mixture in the bowl until it is smooth and pliable. No crumbs should remain. Press the fudge into the prepared pan and sprinkle with the chopped walnuts. Let the fudge sit 30 minutes before cutting into squares for serving.

Makes 1 pound fudge

Cud'n Gwendolyn's
PEANUT BUTTER CANDY

Whenever we asked Cud'n Gwendolyn to bring something sweet to pass, she automatically knew that what we had in mind was her peanut butter candy. It tastes just like the inside of a Butterfinger candy bar.

2 cups chunky peanut butter

1 teaspoon vanilla extract

2 cups granulated sugar

½ cup water

1½ cups light corn syrup

1½ teaspoons baking soda

Grease 2 large baking sheets. Set them aside.

In a large bowl, combine the peanut butter and vanilla extract. Set aside.

In a large, heavy saucepan, combine the sugar and water. Stirring constantly, bring the mixture to a boil over high heat. Decrease the heat slightly and stir in the corn syrup. Let the mixture continue to boil, without stirring, until it reaches 300°F on a candy thermometer. Remove the pan from the heat and quickly but thoroughly stir in the baking soda and the peanut butter mixture. Immediately pour the candy onto the prepared cookie sheets. Using a wooden spoon, spread the candy as thin as possible, then let cool completely. Break the brittle into bite-sized pieces before serving.

Makes about 1 pound candy

WHITE POTATO CANDY

This rich and sweet old-fashioned southern treat is a wonderful way to use up leftover mashed potatoes.

1 russet potato, peeled

4 cups confectioners' sugar

1 teaspoon vanilla extract

½ cup crunchy peanut butter

In a saucepan, cover the potato with water. Bring to a boil and cook until the potato is soft, about 15 to 20 minutes. Drain the potato and let cool. Place the potato in a large bowl and mash with a fork. Gradually add the confectioners' sugar and the vanilla extract. Stir until the mixture has a doughy consistency. Roll the dough out into a rectangle about ¼ inch thick, on waxed paper or on a surface dusted with confectioners' sugar. Spread the peanut butter thinly onto the dough. Roll the dough into a tight, jelly roll–like loaf. Wrap the roll in waxed paper or plastic wrap and refrigerate until it hardens enough to slice. Slice the roll into pieces ½ inch thick and serve.

Makes 1 pound candy

Left, Aint Marjell; *right,* Aint Betty Jean, early 1960s. Betty Jean's wedding and reception took place inside My My and Pop's large house. All the food for the wedding was home-cooked.

Miss Trimbley's
STOVE-TOP PEANUT BRITTLE

Cud'n Eunice cleaned house for a rich white woman in Mississippi named Mrs. Trimbley. No sooner than Mrs. Trimbley set out each morning on her daily round of card games and coffee, Cud'n Eunice would fix herself a tall glass of ice tea (using Miss Trimbley's company crystal) and a nice little sandwich snack; then she'd sit down and copy tons of Mrs. Trimbley's heirloom family recipes. About 30 minutes before Mrs. Trimbley was due back, Cud'n Eunice would put the recipes back in their hiding places, then she'd tousle herself up like she'd been working hard all day. Cud'n Eunice was a mess.

2 cups granulated sugar

1 cup light corn syrup

1 cup water

½ teaspoon salt

4 cups shelled, raw peanuts, with the skins on

3 tablespoons unsalted butter

1 teaspoon vanilla extract

1½ teaspoons baking soda, sifted

Grease 2 large cookie sheets. Set them aside.

In a large, heavy saucepan, bring the sugar, corn syrup, water, and salt to a rapid boil over medium-high heat. Add the peanuts. Continue cooking until the mixture reaches 295°F on a candy thermometer. Remove the pan from the heat and add the butter, vanilla extract, and baking soda. Beat the ingredients rapidly until well mixed. Pour the mixture onto the prepared cookie sheets. Spread the candy to a ¼-inch thickness. Let it cool. Break the brittle into large pieces before serving.

Note: If you can't find shelled, raw peanuts with the skins on, it's fine to substitute shelled, raw peanuts without skins.

Makes about 2 pounds candy

Cud'n Merle's
MISSISSIPPI BEAN FUDGE

They say Cud'n Merle wasn't inclined to give out her recipes. Truth be told, Cud'n Merle wasn't inclined to give out compliments either. They say she was the most envious woman you'd ever want to meet. Instead of telling you "That's pretty" or "That's nice," the way most folks would when you showed them something new, when you showed Cud'n Merle something that you'd just bought she'd look at the thing sideways, roll her eyes, then grunt and say, " Hmmp! I'll catch up to you one of these days."

They say Cud'n Merle had a house full of junk because of her envy; said it was so crowded in the place you had to walk sideways to maneuver through the rooms to keep from tripping. They say Cud'n Merle died trying to keep up with the proverbial Joneses. Said she worked herself to the bone because she didn't want anybody to outdo her. My My used to say, " Where there's envy, there's strife."

Richly flavored and sweet, Cud'n Merle's bean fudge doesn't taste one bit like beans.

1½ cups canned butter beans, drained

½ cup evaporated milk

2 cups granulated sugar

½ cup light corn syrup

1½ cups milk chocolate chips

1½ cups miniature marshmallows

2 tablespoons cornstarch

1 cup confectioners' sugar

½ cup chopped pecans

Grease a 9 by 13-inch square pan. Set it aside.

In a large bowl, mash the beans until they resemble mashed potatoes in texture. Set the beans aside.

In a large saucepan over medium heat, bring the milk, sugar, and corn syrup to a boil. Cook, stirring constantly, until the mixture reaches 238°F degrees on a candy thermometer. Add the butter beans, stirring constantly to mash out any lumps that may form, and bring the mixture back up to 238°F degrees on a candy thermometer. Be very careful: the mixture is extremely hot. Stir in the chocolate chips until they are completely melted. Add the marshmallows and stir until they are completely melted. Remove the pan from the heat and add the cornstarch, stirring vigorously to ensure that it is evenly distributed. Let cool for 2 to 3 minutes. Add the confectioners' sugar and pecans, stirring vigorously until they are completely mixed in. Pour the fudge into the prepared pan. Let the fudge cool completely. Cut it into squares before serving.

Makes about 2 pounds fudge

CRACKER CANDY

This old-timey candy made with saltine crackers will remind you of Almond Roca. It's one of my favorites.

35 to 40 saltine crackers

1 cup (2 sticks) unsalted butter

½ cup firmly packed light brown sugar

½ cup firmly packed dark brown sugar

12 ounces semisweet chocolate chips

1½ cups coarsely chopped pecans or walnuts

Preheat the oven to 350°F.

Line a small baking sheet with aluminum foil. Spray the surface with a nonstick cooking spray. Arrange the crackers evenly on the foil. In a heavy saucepan, melt the butter. Add the light and dark brown sugars to the butter. Bring the mixture to a boil for 3 minutes, or until it becomes thick. Pour the sugar mixture evenly over the crackers. Use a spatula to make sure all of the crackers are covered with the mixture. Bake the crackers for 5 to 7 minutes. Remove the crackers from the oven and sprinkle with the chocolate chips and the nuts. Return the mixture to the oven until the chips are melted enough to spread. Lightly spread the melted chips and nuts over the crackers until they form an even coating. Refrigerate the candy until it is set and break into bite-sized pieces for serving.

Makes 4 to 5 dozen pieces candy

Po' Cud'n Ophelia's
OLD-FASHIONED PECAN CANDY

Cud'n Ophelia—Pop's first cousin—never married. She attended all of our family picnics and holiday dinners without a man. In an era when a woman's estimation hinged upon her ability to catch and keep a man, Cud'n Ophelia stood out like a rose in a bed of daisies. The women in my family spoke of her situation in hushed, sympathetic tones, as if she had some sort of infirmity; as far back as I can remember, My My referred to her as "Po' 'Phelia" because of it. Despite the fact that she owned a successful little alterations shop, drove a New Yorker, and kept a lovely brick home on the west side of town, as far as My My was concerned, Cud'n Ophelia's worldly accomplishments paled against the fact that she didn't have a husband. In those days, unmarried men were called eligible bachelors, while unmarried women were called spinsters and old maids. My My was always on the lookout, always asking somebody if they knew a nice eligible bachelor to introduce to Po' Cud'n 'Phelia. My My even had us kids on the lookout.

Cud'n Ophelia's pecan brittle was thin and crunchy and chock-full of nuts. Cud'n Ophelia loved pecans; she was known to increase the amount of pecans called for in the recipe to 3 cups.

---

1 cup light corn syrup

2¼ cups granulated sugar

1 cup water

2 cups chopped pecans

2 tablespoons unsalted butter

½ teaspoon salt

1 teaspoon baking soda, sifted

2 teaspoons vanilla extract

Generously grease 2 cookie sheets. Set them aside.

Combine the corn syrup, sugar, and water in a heavy saucepan. Blend well. Bring to a boil over medium-high heat, stirring to dissolve the sugar. Lower the heat to a simmer. Continue cooking without stirring until the mixture registers 250°F on a candy thermometer. Stir in the pecans. Continue cooking, stirring occasionally, until the mixture registers 300°F on a candy thermometer. Remove from the heat. Gently stir in the butter, salt, baking soda, and vanilla extract. Working quickly, pour the mixture onto the prepared cookie sheets and spread as thinly as possible. The more you spread it, the crunchier it will be. Let the sheets cool completely on wire racks. Break the brittle into pieces for serving.

Makes about 2 pounds candy

My My's

PRALINES

Most pralines are prepared by dropping the candy by teaspoonfuls onto a strip of waxed paper or aluminum foil to harden. My My's recipe instructs you to pour the candy mixture into a baking pan, in order to cut it into squares after it's set.

1½ cups firmly packed dark brown sugar

1½ cups granulated sugar

1 cup heavy cream

3 tablespoons dark corn syrup

½ cup (1 stick) unsalted butter

1 teaspoon vanilla extract

1 teaspoon maple-flavored extract

4½ cups pecans halves

Grease a 9-inch square pan. Set it aside.

Combine the brown and white sugars, the cream, and the corn syrup in a large, heavy saucepan. Bring the mixture to a boil over low to medium heat. Stir constantly, scraping the bottom and the sides of the saucepan with a long-handled wooden spoon, until a drop of the mixture forms a soft ball when dropped into a cup of ice-cold water and the mixture reaches 238°F on a candy thermometer. Remove the pan from the heat. Add the butter, the vanilla and maple-flavored extracts, and the pecans. Beat the mixture until the pecans are covered and the mixture holds its shape. Pour the candy into the prepared pan. Cool completely on a wire rack. Cut into 1-inch squares before serving.

Makes about 2 pounds candy

Pop and
Aint Helen.

Miss LaLou's
BOURBON BALLS

My My's formal holiday dinners were a big hit. Nothing was more important to My My and Pop than sitting down to a large meal with family. Just before the big day (Easter Sunday, Thanksgiving, Christmas, or New Year's Day), My My would starch her fancy tablecloth and matching napkins until they were crisp enough to stand up on their own. She polished and shined her gold-plated flatware and gold-rimmed crystal drinking glasses until they sparkled. Pop put the extension in the dining room table, and even though the long table took up the entire room, nobody worried that it wouldn't be covered on the big day. The women in my family believed in having a'plenty. The day and eve before the event, folks— neighbors and church members as well as family—flocked to My My and Pop's house in droves, dropping off plates of side dishes and desserts. My My was real funny, though, about deciding what food to eat. When folks stopped by and when she went to visit, she was ever watchful of people's hand-washing habits. My My accepted some dishes at the front door, skinnin' and grinnin' and talkin' about how well they were gonna go with the rest of the meal, then no sooner than the person delivering the goods stepped off the front porch she carried them straight out the back door and gave them to Pal, Pop's beagle. Pal would eat anybody's cooking; didn't matter to him whether they were clean or nasty. Miss LaLou had everybody's approval when it came to cleanliness. She was so clean that in the summer she gave her white poodle, Sugar, a soapy sponge bath in the front yard every day. Of course, the women in my family said that those baths that Miss LaLou gave Sugar were excuses for her to flirt with the men passing by. Our family sure looked forward to the holidays, and to Miss LaLou's bourbon balls.

---

3 cups crushed vanilla wafers

1½ cups chopped pecans

1½ cups confectioners' sugar, plus more for dusting

¼ cup unsweetened cocoa powder

¼ cup light corn syrup

¼ to ½ cup bourbon

1 tablespoon vanilla extract

In a large bowl, combine the wafers, pecans, confectioners' sugar, and cocoa powder. Mix the ingredients until they are well blended. In a small bowl, combine the corn syrup and bourbon. Add the vanilla extract and mix well. Pour the bourbon mixture into the crushed wafer mixture. Blend the ingredients well with a fork. Let the mixture sit for 1 to 2 hours. Taste the mixture. If you like, you can add up to another ¼ cup bourbon at this point, making sure the mixture is not too moist to form into balls. If the mixture is too dry to roll easily, add more corn syrup. Shape tablespoonfuls of the mixture into 1-inch balls. Roll the balls in confectioners' sugar to coat. Arrange the balls on waxed paper and allow to stand several hours to dry a little. You may eat these right away, but they taste much better if you allow them to age in an airtight container in the refrigerator for at least 2 days.

Makes about 4 dozen balls

Left to right: My My's sisters Evelyn and Bulah sitting on the back porch of Aint Bulah's grocery store.

Ice Cream

Aint Marjell working at Cooks restaurant.

$\mathcal{I}$ have wonderful ice cream memories.

If my love of ice cream began anywhere, I would say it began at home with Mama and Daddy. Almost every Sunday during the hot summer, Daddy would drive Mama and me to the ice cream parlor around the corner from our house. Sometimes we'd drive around our little town, window shopping from the car and licking our vanilla ice cream cones, but most times Daddy would park in the parlor's lot and we'd lick our cones amid other ice-cream-cone-licking families. Sometimes, Daddy, Mama, and I walked to the parlor; Mama wore colorful pearls, a matching sundress, and heels. Daddy wore his suit.

There is something about summertime that makes ice cream taste especially good, but in my family, ice cream was more than just a sweet taste of summer; it was a taste that we craved all year long. Even in the winter, Mama bought ice cream by the gallon. She found many ways to serve it: on top of pies or cobblers, in rainbow-colored cones, and sometimes in bowls, topped with one of her home-canned fruit syrups.

I can't think of anyone in our family who didn't like ice cream. My grandparents considered ice cream a wholesome evening treat. When we kids gathered at My My's house for sleep-overs, the highlight of the evening was when Pop reached inside his trouser pocket and pulled out a palmful of coins. We knew instantly what that meant: one of the big kids would be sent down the street to the ice cream parlor inside Cooks restaurant for a tub of soda fountain ice cream. Pop would stand on the sidewalk in front of the house to watch for cars and to give the signal when it was okay to cross busy Sixth Street. When Aint Marjell—she cooked and waited tables at Cooks—was working the ice cream counter she filled our tub with heaping scoops.

Of course, there were also the summer days when we'd be sitting on My My and Pop's porch steps, playing a game of rock school or Chinese checkers, when suddenly the jingle of bells in the distance caught someone's attention. Everyone got vigorously quiet. Sure enough! It *was* the ice cream man coming by foot. Judging from the sound of the bells on his three-wheeled cart, he was far enough away that we had just enough time to run inside and collect dimes from our grandparents. Naturally, when the ice cream man stopped in front of the house, Pop stood on the porch to watch over the transactions.

Ice cream socials were also very popular when I was a little girl. The schools in our community sponsored at least two socials a year. It was such a treat to come home and find a flyer announcing the ice cream social sitting on the kitchen table, or to have one of my cousins call to say that he or she had come home to find such a treasure. Pop usually walked us to the socials. Even though this meant that we couldn't run around wild, the way the kids who came without parents could, we still had a good time. Pop allowed each of us two pastel-colored cupcakes to go along with our sundaes and floats and miniature tubs packed with vanilla ice cream, with a small wooden spoon glued to the top.

When I was five, a man Daddy was paying to do carpentry work on our porch steps put down his saw long enough to buy cherry Popsicles for me and Mama from the ice cream man who was walking by. Daddy wasn't amused. He didn't look twice at the cherry Popsicle that the man bought for me; it was the one he bought for Mama that Daddy wasn't too tickled about. In those days, you just didn't go around buying another man's wife a cherry Popsicle.

Homemade ice cream—now that was something that was out of this world. It was a special treat that made even the most ordinary day seem special. When someone in the family called to say they'd made homemade ice cream, it was an event. We got to that person's house as quickly as we could, even if that meant we'd have to travel clear to Flint, Michigan—thirty-five miles away—to get to Aint Helen's house.

As far as I'm concerned, Aint Helen made the best homemade ice cream (Mama gave that honor to Aint Bulah). The thing that made Aint Helen's ice cream so good was that she made it with her husband in mind; ice cream was something he truly loved. And like I've said, Aint Helen was one of those women who cooked to please her man. If her husband liked something, Aint Helen *put her foot in it* whenever she cooked it.

I feel blessed to have the wonderful ice cream (and Popsicle) memories that I have. I feel even more blessed to have the *homemade* ice cream memories that I have. If you've ever tasted ice cream made the old-fashioned way, you'll know what I mean; there's just no comparison to even the best-tasting store-bought brands.

My My's
SNOW ICE CREAM

This treat from Mississippi was something we looked forward to during or immediately after a fresh snowfall. While the snow was still coming down, My My would send us out back with large mixing bowls and tell us to collect only the whitest snow. Nothing compared to the excitement we felt as we hurried into our snowsuits, then out the door. Of course, back then the air was pure and fresh, not like it is today. These days, with the air quality in many areas being so poor, I'd be careful where I gathered my snow.

1½ gallons fresh, clean snow

½ cup cold evaporated milk

3 cups cold whole milk

1 cup granulated sugar

1 teaspoon vanilla extract

Collect fresh and clean snow in a large pan. Set the pan aside. In a large bowl, combine the evaporated and whole milk, sugar, and vanilla extract, mixing well. Pour the mixture over the snow. Stir briefly, until the snow has absorbed the mixture. Serve immediately in chilled bowls.

Note: To make this treat the snow must be fluffy, not hard and icy or wet and heavy.

Makes about 1 gallon

My My's maternal grandmother, Dicey Evans. Rural Mississippi, early 1900s.

VANILLA ICE CREAM

Chopped fruits—fresh or dried—and chopped nuts make a wonderful topping for a bowl of homemade ice cream.

1 vanilla bean

2 cups milk

5 egg yolks

1¼ cups granulated sugar

2 cups heavy cream

1 teaspoon vanilla extract

With a sharp knife, cut the vanilla bean in half lengthwise. With the tip of the knife, scrape the tiny seeds into a saucepan. Add the split bean and milk and bring to a gentle boil. Cover the saucepan and remove it from the heat. Let the mixture steep for 40 minutes. In a large bowl, beat the egg yolks and sugar until the mixture is light and thick, 3 to 5 minutes. Return the saucepan containing the milk to a simmer over low heat. Remove the vanilla bean. Add a bit of the milk mixture to the egg yolk mixture, temper it, then add the egg yolk mixture to the milk. Stir constantly with a wooden spoon until it is well blended. Remove the pan from the heat when the mixture is thick enough to coat the back of the wooden spoon. Cover and refrigerate until well chilled, about 3 hours or overnight. Stir in the heavy cream and vanilla extract. Freeze the mixture in a 2-quart ice cream maker according to the manufacturer's directions.

Makes about 1 ¹/₂ quarts

OLD-FASHIONED PEACH ICE CREAM

When I was growing up, our entire family picnicked at the park on the old Bay City Highway on week-ends and summer holidays. The Saginaw River, which ran the length of the park, provided a beautiful backdrop. Our picnics were action-packed events involving gigantic beach balls, spirited games of bid-whist, energetic softball games, and animated storytelling. And of course there were huge wooden baskets filled with fried chicken, large buckets of potato salad, and foot-long coolers stuffed with chipped ice and an assortment of pastel-colored soft drinks. Despite how delightful all the food was, the high point of the day occurred when someone cracked open the ice cream freezer and started scooping out servings of someone's luscious homemade ice cream. Peach was one of my favorites.

7 peaches, peeled, pitted, and coarsely chopped

1 teaspoon vanilla extract

1 tablespoon fresh lemon juice

1½ cups granulated sugar

1 cup milk

3 cups heavy cream

In a large bowl, using a potato masher, mash the peaches into a coarse pulp. Stir in the vanilla extract, lemon juice, and ½ cup of the sugar. Let the mixture stand for 1 hour at room temperature. After an hour, add the milk and the remaining 1 cup sugar. Mix well. Cover and refrigerate until it is well chilled, about 3 hours. Remove from refrigerator, stir to blend, and stir in the cream. Pour the custard into the canister of a 2-quart ice cream maker and freeze according to the manufacturer's instructions.

Makes about 1½ quarts

Aint Helen, old Bay City High-way, early 1960s.

Left to right: My cousin Jerry, Mama, me, my cousin David, my cousin Bernard, my cousin Larry. My My's front porch, late 1950s.

Everyday Kool-Aid

When I was growing up, Kool-Aid was the drink of choice in our neighborhood. It was cheap—ten cents a packet—it was sugary, and it stretched a long way. Daddy made a pitcherful every day. Of course it was Mama who added the garnish to make it look pretty.

> Granulated sugar, as needed
> Water, as needed
> 1 package of Kool-Aid
> 2 tablespoons fresh or reconstituted lemon juice
> Orange slices for garnish
> Ice cubes

Add sugar and water to the Kool-Aid as directed on the package. Stir in the lemon juice and add a bit more sugar, if desired. Garnish with orange slices and serve over ice.

Makes 2 quarts

Cud'n Bay Bay's
BUTTERMILK ICE CREAM

Cud'n Bay Bay's buttermilk ice cream was the best! The faint taste of cinnamon made this cool treat a definite crowd pleaser.

6 egg yolks

1¼ cups granulated sugar

3 cups buttermilk

1½ cups heavy cream

⅛ teaspoon ground cinnamon

1 teaspoon vanilla extract

In a bowl, beat together the egg yolks and sugar until they are well blended. Pour the mixture into the top of a double boiler. Stir in the buttermilk, cream, cinnamon, and vanilla extract. Cook the mixture over simmering water, stirring constantly, until it thickens, about 15 minutes. Do not allow to reach a boil. Remove the mixture from the heat and strain through a sieve into a large bowl. Cover the bowl and refrigerate until the mixture is well chilled, about 3 hours. Transfer the custard to the canister of a 2-quart ice cream maker and freeze according to the manufacturer's instructions.

Makes about 1½ quarts

Left, Mama, in black dress; *right,* Bay Bay, in white dress, 1940s. When their chores were done, the women would gather their kids and head up to the Bay City Highway for an afternoon of woman talk.

GOOD OL' STRAWBERRY ICE CREAM

When I tell folks that I've been working off and on since I was four years old, I'm not exaggerating. Shortly after we moved to the outskirts of town, Mama, who was searching our two acres of property for a suitable garden site, stumbled upon a few wild strawberry seedlings. Excited, she carefully dug up the young plants, gave me a quick lesson in botanical essences (Mama was a hippie way before the idea caught on), and then quickly agreed to pay me a nickel for each baby strawberry plant that I could subsequently find. Of course I started my new job with all of the gusto that most of us have when we begin a new career. Mama would stand at the door, hand me my little tin pail and a big tablespoon, and wish me success. "Don't forget to dig all the way down to the roots," she'd remind. "We can't replant if we don't have the roots."

Eventually, my enthusiasm for my strawberry job waned. Some days Mama coaxed me into going to work, especially when I looked bored or unhappy (at that point, I hadn't made friends in our new neighborhood). Mama would say, "Don't forget about my strawberry patch. I just need a few more seedlings and then I'll have enough to make a nice little row. Nobody can find strawberry seedlings better than you; you got an eye for it."

Now that I'm grown, I'm sure there was some virtue that Mama was trying to instill in me—an honorable work ethic, a discernment for God's bountiful grace and provision, something. More than the nickel Mama gave me for each seedling that I brought her, what I recollect most is the smile on her face and the gleam in her eyes when she'd look inside my pail. "Would you look at that," she'd say. "You found two more plants. I don't know what I'd do without you; you have such a keen eye." Even today, that smile, that gleam, Mama's approval, influences every thing that I do.

---

4 eggs, beaten

1½ cups granulated sugar

2 tablespoons cornstarch

½ teaspoon salt

5 cups whole milk

1 (13-ounce) can evaporated milk

1 (14-ounce) can sweetened condensed milk

1 tablespoon vanilla extract

4 cups fresh strawberries, hulled and mashed or puréed

In a large bowl, beat the eggs, sugar, cornstarch, and salt until the mixture is completely blended. Set the bowl aside. In a large saucepan, heat the milk over medium heat just until it reaches a boil. Immediately reduce the heat to low and temper the egg mixture by adding a bit of hot milk to it, then slowly add the egg mixture to the hot milk, beating constantly. Cook until the custard thickens, about 15 minutes. Remove the custard from the heat and allow it to cool in the refrigerator for at least 3 hours. Stir in the evaporated milk, sweetened condensed milk, and vanilla extract. Add the mashed or puréed strawberries and mix well. Pour the custard into the canister of a 4-quart ice cream maker and freeze according to the manufacturer's instructions.

Makes about 2½ quarts

Aint Tee's
LUSCIOUS LEMON ICE CREAM

"Aint Tee" was what we called My My's sister, Laura. Aint Tee wasn't too quick to give out her recipes . . . not even to family. In fact, if she agreed to give you a recipe, you had to agree to give her one back. Aint Tee traded recipes the way we children traded paper dolls and marbles.

This ice cream has a soft, smooth texture and it tastes lemony delicious. I like to fix myself a heaping bowl covered in raspberry sauce.

---

3 egg yolks

2 cups granulated sugar

1 tablespoon cornstarch

1 cup milk

½ cup fresh lemon juice

2 cups heavy cream

½ tablespoon grated lemon zest

In a large, heavy saucepan whisk together the egg yolks, sugar, cornstarch, milk, and lemon juice. Cook the mixture over medium heat, whisking constantly, until a candy thermometer registers 175°F, about 15 minutes. Do not allow to boil. Strain the mixture through a sieve into a bowl and cool in the refrigerator for at least 3 hours. Add the cream and the lemon zest to the cooled lemon curd and mix well. Pour the custard into the canister of a 2-quart ice cream maker and freeze according to the manufacturer's instructions.

Makes about 1½ quarts

My My's mother, Ella Dixon. We called her Lil' Mama. For years she lived in New Orleans. But in later years (as shown here), she longed for rural Mississippi, her birthplace. So against everyone's wishes, she moved back.

Real Old-Fashioned Lemonade

I can still picture it. We'd be sitting on the porch watching the people and the cars go by; My My would get up and go inside the house. In a short while the screen door would squeak on its hinges as she returned with a tray containing tall glasses and a big pitcher of homemade lemonade. "This is a heap better'n that store-bought stuff," Pop would say, after his first gulp. We kids would take a big gulp, then nod our heads and agree.

> 7 lemons, at room temperature, plus 1 lemon for garnish
> 1½ cups granulated sugar
> Ice cubes
> Water, as needed

Thinly slice 1 lemon and set it aside for garnish. Roll the remaining 7 lemons on a hard, flat surface. Slice each lemon in half, then squeeze the juice into a gallon container. Toss the lemon rinds into the container. Pour the sugar over the rinds and let stand for 30 minutes. Add the ice cubes and enough water to fill the container. Stir. Garnish glasses with the lemon slices and fill with lemonade.

Makes 4 quarts

DOWN-HOME BANANA ICE CREAM

This was Aint Helen's recipe. Nobody, and I do mean nobody, could make a better ice cream than Aint Helen. Sometimes she'd add about a cup and a half of chopped nuts before freezing; sometimes she'd add them afterward. Either way, plain or crunchy, when we were invited to Aint Helen's for banana ice cream we went with a smile.

2 cups milk

2 cups heavy cream

4 eggs, beaten

1½ cups granulated sugar

¼ teaspoon salt

4 very ripe bananas, mashed

1 teaspoon vanilla extract

1 tablespoon fresh lemon juice

⅛ teaspoon ground nutmeg

In a large saucepan, combine the milk, cream, eggs, granulated sugar, and salt. Cook over low heat, stirring constantly, until the mixture thickens slightly and coats the back of a wooden spoon, about 10 minutes. Refrigerate the mixture in a covered bowl for at least 3 hours. Meanwhile, in a large bowl, sir the bananas, vanilla extract, lemon juice, and nutmeg together until smooth. Stir the cooled custard into the banana mixture. Pour the custard into the canister of a 2-quart ice cream maker and freeze according to the manufacturer's instructions.

Makes about 1½ quarts

Big Mama's
SODA POP ICE CREAM FLOAT

This summer classic proves that a dessert doesn't have to be complicated to be delicious.

2 large scoops plus 1 small scoop vanilla ice cream

1 (8-ounce) can root beer or cola

Spoon the 2 large scoops of vanilla ice cream into a tall mug or tumbler. Slowly pour the root beer over the ice cream, taking care not to spill the soda over the top of the container. Gently stir to mix. Add the small scoop of ice cream on top. Serve with a long-handled spoon.

Serves 1

Southern-Style Sun Tea

The best thing to quench your thirst on a hot summer day.

4 tea bags
1½ quarts cold water
Granulated sugar, to taste
Ice cubes

Place the tea bags in a 2-quart clear glass container. Add the water. Cover the container and let it stand in the hot sun for 3 to 4 hours, or until the tea reaches the desired strength. Remove the tea bags. Add sugar to suit your taste, then serve over ice.

Makes 1½ quarts

Front-Porch Treats

Sitting on the porch in the summertime, especially at My My's house in the old neighborhood, was one of our favorite pastimes. Between Mama, My My, my aunts, and me, we knew a little bit of something about everybody in the neighborhood.

"Don't look now, but that's so and so's ol' uppity daughter, so and so, comin' up the street. That gal wouldn't speak to you if she was sittin' in your lap." My My thought it was a disgrace for someone to pass the porch without asking, *How ya'll doin' today?* "You can say what you wanna say 'bout the country," she would fuss beneath her breath, "but at least where I come from, folks know'd they manners."

I learned many of life's lessons sitting on the front porch in the old neighborhood with Mama, My My, or one of my aunts. Each person who passed by served as inspiration. I saw how bad you could end up looking if you squandered your youth on booze and fast living; saw how men passing in cars smiled and tipped their hats at decent-acting women on their way to market; and heard the trash they hurled out the window at the ones who swished down the street like alley cats in heat. I learned that whether it's right or wrong, people do judge you by your outward appearance: how you walk, how you talk, the company you keep.

When I think of those summer days on the front porch long ago, I think of the clinking of ice cubes in tall rose-patterned glasses and of Mama, My My, my aunts, and the lessons they taught me.

Sweets

Left to right: Cud'n Rachel, Cud'n Daisy, me. Family reunion, rural Mississippi, 1960s.

Big Mama, age seventeen, and her first husband, Sam, 1911.

Afterword

Like Mama used to say, time *does* bring changes. Once the heartbeat of our community, Sixth Street—the way we knew it back then—has been erased. In fact, the entire community, including My My's house, Miss LaLou's house, and Miss Emma Brenyak's house and her dry cleaner, have been bulldozed to make room for progress—Interstate 75. Cud'n Junior, one of my childhood playmates who moved to Atlanta, Georgia, in the early 1970s, came back home a few years ago; he hadn't been home in years. He cried like a baby after he went in search of the old neighborhood and couldn't find even a trace of it. He told everybody that he wouldn't be coming back home none too soon; said it was just too depressing to see everything from his childhood either torn down or boarded up.

Many of the women of my childhood who are responsible for the *who* of what I have become—Mama, My My, Aint Bulah, Aint Jessie Mae, Cud'n Bay Bay, and Big Mama, just to name a few—have gone on to be with the Lord. Time has brought many changes to my life. But, if what they say is true, that we are watched over and prayed for by our ancestors, then I don't feel so bad.

Not too long ago I dreamt that I was walking down an old dirt road with beautiful fruit and vegetable crops growing on either side. There were rows and rows of workers in the fields, each one humming and hoeing in perfect unison. In the distance, a huge Victorian-style mansion stood high on a hill. The closer I got to the pristine mansion, I could feel its importance to the happy field workers. Something spiritual and nourishing radiated from inside its clean walls. The workers smiled lovingly when they looked in the direction of the mansion. When I finally reached the foot of the hill on which the mansion stood, Mama, My My, Aint Jessie Mae, and Big Mama came rushing out to greet me. They were wearing aprons perfumed with the scent of fried chicken, ham hocks, mustard greens, cornbread, and peach cobbler. They invited me inside the house. Once inside, we went straight to the kitchen where they had been preparing a meal for the field workers. They

159

immediately went back to work, stirring and dicing and chopping and kneading. They—including Big Mama—were laughing and joking and having a real good time.

I believe the dream was trying to tell me that it *is* true what they say about heaven: when we go there, we are assigned the things we loved to do on earth. I believe that it's true because the queens of soul food sure looked happy in that big, pristine kitchen in the sky, doing what they'd loved doing best here on earth—cookin' up a storm.

The women of my family, 1960s.

Index

641.86
P

Pinner, Patty.

Sweets.

DATE			

24.95   1-21-04

BAKER & TAYLOR